IN THE
NATIONAL INTEREST

General Sir John Monash once exhorted a graduating class to 'equip yourself for life, not solely for your own benefit but for the benefit of the whole community'. At the university established in his name, we repeat this statement to our own graduating classes, to acknowledge how important it is that common or public good flows from education.

Universities spread and build on the knowledge they acquire through scholarship in many ways, well beyond the transmission of this learning through education. It is a necessary part of a university's role to debate its findings, not only with other researchers and scholars, but also with the broader community in which it resides.

Publishing for the benefit of society is an important part of a university's commitment to free intellectual inquiry. A university provides civil space for such inquiry by its scholars, as well as for investigations by public intellectuals and expert practitioners.

This series, In the National Interest, embodies Monash University's mission to extend knowledge and encourage informed debate about matters of great significance to Australia's future.

Professor Margaret Gardner AC
President and Vice-Chancellor,
Monash University

JOHN LYONS

DATELINE JERUSALEM: JOURNALISM'S TOUGHEST ASSIGNMENT

MONASH
UNIVERSITY
PUBLISHING

Monash University Publishing
Matheson Library Annexe
40 Exhibition Walk
Monash University
Clayton, Victoria 3800, Australia
https://publishing.monash.edu

Monash University Publishing brings to the world publications which advance the best traditions of humane and enlightened thought.

ISBN: 9781922464842 (paperback)
ISBN: 9781922464859 (ebook)

Series: In the National Interest
Editor: Louise Adler
Project manager & copyeditor: Paul Smitz
Designer: Peter Long
Typesetter: Cannon Typesetting
Proofreader: Gillian Armitage
Printed in Australia by Ligare Book Printers

A catalogue record for this book is available from the National Library of Australia.

DATELINE JERUSALEM: JOURNALISM'S TOUGHEST ASSIGNMENT

As someone who'd tried to avoid running most of my life, I was surprised to find myself, at the age of fifty-two, pounding along the old railway track in Jerusalem, sweating under the Middle Eastern sun but determined to be ready for the prize fight. Over four months, I'd become the fittest I'd been since I was eighteen. I needed to be: I was about to face the full fury of Australia's pro-Israel lobby. I was busy working on a story, 'Stone Cold Justice',[1] as a guest reporter for *Four Corners*, which I knew the lobby would not like. I knew the hardline supporters in Australia of Israeli settlements in the Palestinian Territories well enough to understand that this story would unleash a propaganda fatwa against me.

I knew that if I reported the truth about the treatment of Palestinian children in the West Bank, I would be the target of a backlash which would be tough, nasty and prolonged. I knew that the report would not encourage a debate about the central theme of the story—whether it was fair that in the West Bank there is one law for Jewish children and one for Palestinian children—but rather a round of attacks on me.

I'd been granted access to 'children's day' at the Israeli military court, when Palestinian children as young as twelve are put on trial before Israeli soldiers, most commonly for throwing stones at either the Israeli army or Jewish settlers. To my Australian eyes, having one law for a Jewish child and another, much harsher law for a Palestinian child, in the same geographic area, was worth a story. I would write it with the cooperation of the Israeli army and the Israeli Government. But none of that would matter.

When the story aired in February 2014, my peers thought it was good journalism—it won the Walkley Award for best investigative journalism—but I was attacked professionally, personally and relentlessly by the pro-Israel lobby and its supporters. I'd known how fickle many of Israel's supporters in Australia could be. When I'd been a reporter on Channel Nine's *Sunday* program, a prominent member of the Melbourne Jewish community had written to thank me for my 'integrity, morality and courage' after I did a story about threats to Jewish schools which resulted in extra funding for security. But that very same person would turn against me when I was based in Jerusalem and did a story he did not like. Suddenly I was no longer a journalist of integrity, I was 'Goebbels'. He wrote to tell me I was 'a Hamas smelly used tampon'. Someone else wrote: 'Fuck yourself John, why don't you crawl back into a cave with Hamas where you belong.' Six days later, that person followed up with: 'Can't single Jews out forever Lyons as world history has shown that Jews and Israel have outlived their enemies like the scum that you are.' Those comments were but a few of the hundreds I received.

Most journalists based in Jerusalem who report exactly what they see in front of them are trolled and abused. As an indication of how far right much of the pro-Israel lobby has leant, correspondents of *The New York Times*—traditionally one of the newspapers most supportive of Israel—have been systematically targeted. Jodi Rudoren, who was from an observant American Jewish family and who came to Jerusalem to report for that paper when I was there, was attacked even before she landed in Israel. Her crime? After she was announced as the new *NYT* correspondent, an Arab-American sent her a note of congratulations. She replied with a thank you in Arabic: '*Shukran*.'[2] For that, she became a target. Later, a prominent US-based pro-Israel lobby group branded her 'a Nazi bitch'.

One of Rudoren's predecessors, another distinguished Jewish reporter, Clyde Haberman, said in 2014 that every *NYT* correspondent based in Israel had been subjected to non-stop assault and therefore few on the paper would apply for the job, knowing the kicking that their reputation would take. He was reported as saying:

We've had decades of correspondents that, no matter how different they've been one from the other, no matter how talented they are or how many Pulitzer Prizes they have to their name, always end up being accused of being either anti-Semites or self-hating Jews. At some point, this seeps into the DNA of the newspaper. This is what you can expect if you go there—to have your integrity hurled back in your face every single day.[3]

But, with a touch of sarcasm, Haberman said he'd discovered how to placate Israeli hardliners: 'If I didn't want to be accused of hating Israel, I should start every story with: "Fifty years after six million Jews died in the Holocaust, Israel yesterday did one thing or the other."'

As for my *Four Corners* report, although I was expecting attacks, I was surprised that they began even before the story was broadcast. Several hours before it aired, I was sitting in the Sydney office of executive producer Sue Spencer when her inbox began pinging—email after email complaining about the story. Spencer replied to each one: 'Could I please suggest that you wait until the program goes to air until you lodge a complaint.' Whatever complaints could be made were made—they complained to the Australian Communications and Media Authority, to the ABC's managing director and the ABC's chair. All complaints would be dismissed, but while I'd spent two months working on the story, I would spend three months defending it.

Having lived with these sorts of attacks for many years—and this book will lead to a new round—I believe that they are a deliberate tactic. I think the aim is to make journalists and editors decide that, even if they have a legitimate story that may criticise Israel, it is simply not worth running it as it will cause 'more trouble than it's worth'. As the legendary Agence France-Presse correspondent Philippe Agret says, the aim is to 'exhaust' journalists and editors so that they think twice before writing anything critical of Israel.

Over my time as a journalist and editor at several media organisations, I've written or approved a lot of stories that have upset a lot of powerful people. As the editor of *The Sydney Morning Herald*, I dismayed both major party leaders in Australia at that time—John Howard and Paul Keating—along with a few others as well, such as Kerry Packer. Keating and Packer were the most ferocious, but Howard was not far behind. He once unleashed on me while we were having pre-dinner drinks at The Lodge over the *SMH*'s coverage of the Mabo and Wik decisions: 'You've murdered me politically in my own hometown.' Keating once got a member of his office to ring me to say that I was editing 'the second most corrupt newspaper in the country'. Keating was outraged by stories we'd been running about his connection to a piggery. 'Please tell your boss that he knows how to wound us,' I told his staffer. 'Please relay to him that we'd either prefer not to be on his list at all or we'd rather be number one—we don't like coming second for anything.' I added: 'Just out of interest, which is the most corrupt newspaper in the country?' His staffer replied: '*The West Australian*.'

But nothing matches the fury of the right-wing supporters of Israel, who are often bundled together and described as 'the pro-Israel lobby'. When I refer to 'the pro-Israel lobby', I include the Israeli Embassy in Canberra, several of the formal lobby groups, and several individuals who are affiliated with these groups—activists who support the continuing expansion of Israeli settlements in the West Bank. Also, when discussing Israel, left and right are not as they are in Australia. In Israel, right-wing means pro-settlements. It means wanting the Israeli Government to encourage as many Israelis as possible to move into the West Bank and become so-called 'settlers'. Despite protestations from many in the lobby that they are always open to a peace agreement, the lobby knows that sending hundreds of thousands of settlers into the West Bank has made a viable Palestinian state far less likely.

This is the story of why many editors and journalists in Australia are in fear of upsetting these people and therefore—in my view—self-censoring. It's the story of how the Israeli–Palestinian issue is the single issue—the only issue—which the media will not cover with the rigour with which it covers every other issue. And, most importantly, it's the story of how the Australian public is being short-changed—denied reliable, factual information about one of the most important conflicts of our time. As Chris Mitchell, former editor-in-chief of *The Australian*, says: 'I made the decision that I wanted to have a Middle East Bureau … because Australia has its own bilateral relationship with Israel and it's been one of the biggest stories in the world since World War II.'

In forty years in journalism, I've dealt with some smart and powerful lobby groups. But none compares to the pro-Israel lobby in Australia. It is formidable, it is well-funded and it is effective. Too effective, in my view. Material which the lobby opposes being published in Australia is routinely published in Israel. Why should Australians not be able to read stories which are readily available inside Israel? The pressure that the lobby places on journalists is well known, but it is something which only tends to be discussed in hushed tones for fear of reprisals. Peter Greste is one of the few senior journalists prepared to discuss it: 'Personally, I think the pressure that the Israeli lobby places on Australian journalists is, frankly, outrageous.'

If, as a journalist or editor, you jump on board with the lobby, you'll be offered free flights to Israel. If they *really* like you, your partner will be invited as well. You'll be put up at the best hotels in Jerusalem, and wined and dined at the most expensive restaurants where you can drink the best vintages from the Golan Heights. Sometimes, editors and journalists in Australia will give in by pulling a story off a website, apologising, or deciding that such reportage is just too hard. Some outlets give the bare minimum coverage—'the Israelis say this and the Palestinians say that ...' In my view, this is so that they can say they cover the topic, but in reality they do not.

The Israeli army even verbalised to me the different tolerance levels for stories published in Israel as opposed to those published abroad. When I wrote a piece for *The Weekend Australian* on the treatment of Palestinian children before the Israeli military court,[4] a precursor to my *Four Corners* story three years later, the Israeli army wanted to speak to me. I met their spokesperson, Captain Arye Shalicar, at a café in Jerusalem. He pulled my article from his pocket and said: 'We have a problem with this.' I asked if there were any factual mistakes in it. 'No,' he replied, 'we're not challenging the accuracy, but our concern is that it's been published outside Israel. If this had appeared in Israel, in *Haaretz* or *Yedioth* [*Ahronoth*], we could live with it. This sort of thing appears quite a lot. But this appeared in Australia.'

As I reported in my book *Balcony over Jerusalem*, Shalicar went on to explain:

> People in Israel are committed to the State of Israel. Either they have moved here because they are committed to Israel or have remained here because they are. So when they read a story about Israeli soldiers and Palestinian children, they read it in the context that whatever they read, it is not going to shake their commitment. But people in Australia may not have the same commitment. So when they read a story like this they may question their support for Israel. If I was sitting in Australia reading this I would think that Israeli soldiers were brutally treating Palestinian children.[5]

When I said nothing, he continued: 'A story like this may damage the view that Australians have of Israel and they don't have the commitment to Israel to go along with that.'

Many Israelis—and Jewish people in Australia—told me they did not question the accuracy of my reports. They said that these sorts of issues were frequently discussed privately. One Israeli who had moved to Jerusalem from Melbourne told me over lunch that the reason some of my reporting was causing 'a stir' in Melbourne was because I was airing 'dirty linen' which was fine to discuss in private but not in public.

Depriving Australians of objective information about Israel and its occupation of the West Bank means they, as citizens, cannot evaluate or question Australia voting for Israel at the United Nations, no matter the issue, or if Australia's continued support of Israel's 54-year occupation meets our values and interests.

Wars between Israel and the Gaza Strip ignite every few years, and because factual information is limited, the causes often are not explained to us. It is not surprising that the issue which has been festering for decades and is cited as one of the main reasons behind the May 2021 Gaza conflict has rarely been reported in Australia. The media that bothered to report it framed it as essentially a real-estate dispute between Palestinians, who lived in the neighbourhood of Sheikh Jarrah in East Jerusalem, and Jews who claimed they lived in and owned those houses in 1948. As *The New York Times* reported: 'The Israeli law allows Jews to reclaim ownership of land they vacated in 1948 but denies Palestinians the right to reclaim the properties they fled from in the same war.'[6]

Most Australians would also not know that in order to achieve a demographic majority in Jerusalem, for decades many of these Palestinians have had their houses in East Jerusalem demolished or occupied. They also don't know that 'About 3000 Palestinians in 200 East Jerusalem properties are living under threat of eviction, according to Peace Now, an anti-occupation advocacy group. It also estimates that about 20 000 Palestinian homes are under threat of demolition ...'[7]

In the Australian media, the military system which rules over every aspect of the Palestinians' lives in the West Bank is rarely mentioned and even more rarely explained. 'Under Israeli military law army commanders have full executive, legislative and judicial authority over 3 million Palestinians living in the West Bank. Palestinians have no say in how this authority is exercised,' says Military Court Watch, a human-rights monitoring group.[8]

Most Australians do not know that Palestinians have inferior civil rights in the West Bank to Israeli settlers living in the same territory. Most Australians do not know that Palestinians live not just in fear of the Israeli army—particularly after dark—but of Jewish settlers, who often attack them or their homes. Rarely are the settlers held accountable by the army—indeed, Israeli human rights groups have numerous videos of settlers attacking Palestinians while soldiers stand by. Some soldiers are, of course, settlers themselves. Most Australians would not know that there are streets in the West Bank where only Israelis can walk and roads on which only Israelis can drive.

Even leaders of the Australian Jewish community, who publicly defend Israel, do not know much of the reality. When I was the Middle East correspondent in Jerusalem for *The Australian*, Albert Dadon, a property developer from Melbourne who founded the Australia Israel Leadership Forum, called me to say he was coming to the city. We decided to go to Hebron, an experience Dadon had not had. Hebron is the only place in the West Bank where a Jewish settlement is completely surrounded by Palestinians—about 500 settlers are encircled by 200 000 Palestinians. It's where you see the occupation at its starkest because few foreigners or Israelis ever go there. There's no public relations or polishing. It's pure, raw, unvarnished occupation.

As we were driving down a hill into Hebron, Dadon asked me why there were so many Palestinian women walking up the hill, many carrying babies, food and water. 'Because they're not allowed to drive on this road,' I replied. Dadon was shocked—he found it hard to believe that there were roads in Hebron, and across the West Bank, where Israelis were allowed to drive but Palestinians were not. As we walked around Hebron, I pointed to other roads where Palestinians were not just forbidden from driving but were not allowed to walk.

Dadon said he wanted to leave. I told him that he should see the Palestinian houses whose front doors had been sealed by the Israeli army, so the owners could not enter or leave by the main street, but he said, 'I've seen enough. I'm upset that all this is being done in my name.' Dadon was silent for most of the drive back to Jerusalem. He would later tell me that the trip had 'opened my eyes', adding: 'This is the dark side of a society that you don't want to face, but when you face it you come out more informed. What I saw that day was not Jewish.'

Dadon's reflections were important. Despite travelling the world and defending Israel and its policies, when Dadon saw the reality he was upset. Most Israelis know this reality as most of them have served in the army, which is compulsory. Most foreign journalists and aid workers also know this reality, as they sometimes travel to Hebron. So affected was Dadon that he rang me two nights later and said he'd had meetings with eight Israeli ministers since our trip and told them all that 'Hebron has to change'. He said five of the ministers agreed and three did not. But the point Dadon did not grasp from a quick trip to Hebron was that it was not just a matter of Hebron changing. The inequality that Dadon saw in Hebron is the reality across the West Bank. An occupier and the occupied are never equal. The same military laws which Dadon saw in Hebron apply to all Palestinians in the West Bank, as does the same power imbalance between armed settlers and unarmed Palestinians, and the same 'Israeli-only' rules that prevent Palestinians from walking or driving along certain roads.

Most Australians would not know that the majority of Palestinians are not able to pray at Al-Aqsa Mosque, the third-holiest Muslim site, and that thousands of Palestinian Christians cannot pray at the Holy Sepulchre, where Jesus is said to be buried, because the Israeli army will not give them permits to visit Jerusalem. The permit system determines where they can go, where they can work, whether they can get access to medical care, and whether they can have equal employment opportunities. Most Australians would not know that hundreds of Bedouins have had their Israeli citizenship cancelled, leaving them stateless.

Most Australians would not know that Israel's legal justification for keeping three million Palestinians in the West Bank under military rule for fifty-four years is the Fourth Geneva Convention of 1950—the same convention that prohibits settlement construction in East Jerusalem and the West Bank. Not only is this an example of cherry-picking international law, but this selective approach only serves to undermine the credibility of the rules-based order established in the aftermath of World War II.

Most Australians would not know that 'the freedom of expression of Palestinians in the West Bank is almost nonexistent', as noted in a report by Israel's Association for Civil Rights. 'Palestinian vigils and demonstrations are defined as illegal assemblies, military and police forces regard them as a threat and the majority of them are dispersed with use of violence, which sometimes leads to fatal consequences.'[9]

Furthermore, most Australians don't know that often during Jewish holidays such as Yom Kippur and Rosh Hashana, the West Bank is closed off. This means that most Palestinians cannot go to work or university inside Israel for many days. Why should one person's religious holiday be another person's lockdown?

Most Australians would not know that in Area C of the Palestinian Territories—the 61 per cent of the West Bank where all the Jewish settlers live—98 per cent of Palestinian building applications are refused by the Israeli army, and that frequently the army will demolish a school, a village, a shed or house on the basis that the Palestinians do not have a permit. Palestinians from the West Bank are not permitted to fly into or out of Israel's international airport, Ben Gurion. Most Australians would not know that Israel controls all the water for the Palestinians and can turn it off—and sometimes does—if water supplies for the Israelis run low.

Most Australians would not know that the Palestinian residents of East Jerusalem are not allowed to vote in Israeli national elections; they can only vote in the local council elections. And most Australians would not know that in 2018, the Israeli Parliament passed the Nation State Law,[10] which formally entrenches Jewish superiority over Israel's Arab population. This law says that 'Israel is the national home of the Jewish people, and that the right to self-determination is unique only to Jewish citizens—in accordance with Article 1 of the law'. If a discriminatory and racist law had been passed entrenching the superior status of white Australians over Indigenous and other Australians, it would have been front-page news in Australia—but not when the equivalent happens in Israel.

~

Something extraordinary is happening right now in the Middle East. After five decades, Israel's occupation is at a tipping point. If a Palestinian state is ever to be created—as voted for by Australia and the world community at the United Nations General Assembly in 1947—these next five years are crucial.

The pro-Israel lobby likes to say that Israel's dispute with the Palestinians is complicated. It's not. It's blindingly simple. In 1967, Israel began an occupation of the West Bank, which was part of the land set aside by the UN for an Arab state which would be formed alongside a Jewish state. The pro-Israel lobby has been spectacularly successful in framing the perception of Israel's strategic and political situation as vulnerable, its people living under constant existential threat from their neighbours—David surrounded by an Arab Goliath.

The reality is completely different. Firstly, Israel has long had peace agreements with its two biggest Arab neighbours, Egypt and Jordan. And in 2020, it signed peace agreements with several other Arab countries. Furthermore—and this is something that Israel does not like to see written—it is the superpower of the Middle East, complete with a major arsenal of nuclear weapons. As Hezbollah in Lebanon and Hamas in Gaza know full well, any attack on Israel will be met with a fierce response. And its neighbours know that not only do they face the most powerful military in the region, it is backed by intelligence, equipment and funding from the most powerful military on earth: that of the United States.

The essence of an occupation is that it should be temporary—under international law, an occupation is intended to be a period during which the occupying power can work out how to stabilise the situation and then hand over to a longer-term solution. After five decades, Israel cannot argue that its occupation of the West Bank is temporary, which means it is in effect a de-facto annexation. And under international law, annexations are illegal.

The reality of what is happening also has major consequences for Israel. Israelis in their fifties and sixties know nothing other than to be an occupying military power. Generations of eighteen-year-old Israelis have been sent into the West Bank to enforce the occupation—generations have grown up with the experience that, as the soldier with a gun, they are the ultimate authority. According to the UN, since 1967 at least 800 000 Palestinians, including children, have been detained by Israel's army and prosecuted in military courts.

Between 500 and 1000 children, on average, are detained each year. All of this continues to shape modern Israel, so much so that more than 1000 former Israeli combat soldiers have formed a group called Breaking the Silence and now chronicle the human rights abuses they committed—or witnessed—against Palestinian civilians.

Some in Israel who want to see an end to the occupation say they wish Australians were better informed, as this could mean Australia's government and its Jewish community could add to the pressure to end the settlements. One of them is leading Israeli journalist Akiva Eldar, who has visited Australia many times and is familiar with groups such as the Australia/Israel & Jewish Affairs Council. He tells me: 'I'm willing to be on record and tell the AIJAC people and the Australian Government that they are playing with my future, that they don't give a shit about my children, it's about their arses. It is annoying because it has nothing to do with the real strategic, existential interests of Israel. Australia should understand that in the US, Israel is a domestic political issue. Australia has to look at its relationship with Israel independently because the US is not innocently looking at it. I tell my Australian friends and family that … even if you tell your government not to interfere, to take a step back and say nothing, this plays into the hands of the Likud.'

Eldar stresses that 'there is a clear distinction between supporting Israel and supporting the Israeli Government and Israeli policy. If Australia voted in favour of a Palestinian state along 1967 lines, it would be very difficult for the Israeli Government to smear them and say they are anti-Semites because you have a very clean record.'

~

Power. Everyone has a different definition. For me, it's the ability to effect change. If you're a lobbyist, for example, power is the ability to influence the media to give your product, or cause, more favourable coverage than it would otherwise get if you were not expending time and money.

I saw unadulterated power in February 2017. While visiting Sydney, Israel's then prime minister Benjamin Netanyahu had a briefing with editors from major newspapers. During the briefing, he talked mostly about settlements—as a right-winger, Netanyahu's priority was to keep encouraging as many new settlements in the West Bank as possible, to create 'Eretz Israel'—'Greater Israel'. The majority of the Israeli Parliament now supports settlement expansion—many Knesset members are quite open about their view that if enough Jewish settlers populate the West Bank, a Palestinian state becomes physically impossible. That, in turn, means Israel expands to formally include the West Bank—or Greater Israel.

The power I witnessed was captured in an email at 11.54 a.m. on 24 February. It was sent by Colin

Rubenstein, the head of AIJAC, to the editors of *The Australian*. Under the heading 'Netanyahu and settlements', Rubenstein told the editors that 'you can't use what he [Netanyahu] said there'—he wanted to make sure that what Netanyahu said at the briefing remained a secret.

Israel and its supporters call the expansion of settlements 'facts on the ground'. The general view of the lobby is that Israel would genuinely like to see a Palestinian state. This is not true. Poll after poll shows that the majority of Israelis do not favour a two-state solution. A comprehensive poll jointly conducted in 2020 by the Evens Program in Mediation and Conflict Management at Tel Aviv University and the Palestinian Centre for Policy and Survey Research found that only 42 per cent of Israeli Jews supported one. Ominously, the poll also found that attitudes were hardening among young people—while 60 per cent of Israeli Jews over aged over fifty-five supported a two-state solution, this fell to 38 per cent for 35–54-year-olds and to 28 per cent for 18–34-year-olds.[11]

It was no coincidence that the issue Netanyahu was discussing in his private briefing with newspaper editors was settlements. The reason Israel and its lobby groups are so sensitive about settlements is that under international law they are illegal. Article 49 of the Fourth Geneva Convention states: 'The Occupying Power shall not deport or transfer parts of its own civilian population into the territory it occupies.' In my six years of reporting from Jerusalem, from 2009 to 2015, it was when I wrote about settlements that I most came under attack. Unquestionably, Israel is involved in transferring its civilian population into the occupied West Bank. One only needs to drive around the West Bank to see demountable housing and construction materials being transported there from 'Israel proper'. One of the reasons the Fourth Geneva Convention stipulated that civilian populations should not be transferred into occupied territories was to protect those populations—obviously, transporting civilians into an area occupied by a foreign army could be putting them in harm's way. This is not the case, however, with the 800 000 Jewish settlers, as they have the Israeli army to protect them, as well as their own settler security groups.

I remember reading Rubenstein's email and thinking how extraordinary it was. Having made clear the rule, Rubenstein went on to offer an alternative—what the editors *were* allowed to report:

> While you can't use what he [Netanyahu] said there, I thought you might be interested in the attached fact sheet AIJAC has prepared on the subject—which even includes a good map of the sort Netanyahu was complaining he did not have. Anyway, you are welcome to use any or all of the factsheet in any way that you see fit.

The editors abided by Rubenstein's instruction and did not publish a word of what Netanyahu had said at the briefing. Rubenstein signed off his email with the words: 'Thanks again for the wonderfully warm and informative coverage *The Australian* has provided of Netanyahu's visit. All the best, Colin.'

Those interested in a vibrant, open media should think about that email. A lobbyist is telling the editors of a national newspaper that they cannot quote what a foreign leader says to a briefing of editors and journalists—instead, they are 'welcome' to use a 'fact sheet' provided by that lobby group. What gives a lobby group the power to say this? It's worth pointing out that Rubenstein is not an elected official. The Executive Council of Australian Jewry is the elected representative body of Australian Jewry. AIJAC is a privately funded lobby group which over decades has been supported largely by Melbourne corporate lawyer Mark Leibler.

Now let's return to Colin Rubenstein's 'you can't use that' email. I know *The Australian* well. I therefore know that any other lobby group, or country, which tries telling the editors of that paper what they can or cannot report would be treated with the contempt that an interfering lobby group deserves. The European Union couldn't get away with it. The United States couldn't get away with it. Even the Australian prime minister couldn't get away with it. The editors of the News Corp flagship would rise up against anyone else laying down the rules. But not Israel and AIJAC. This showed the potency of AIJAC. Over decades, Rubenstein has built up such a reputation in the country's newsrooms that he can exercise that sort of power. In my experience, very few editors or journalists will say no to Rubenstein, the only lobbyist in the country known only by his first name. 'You don't even need to say "Colin who?",' says Chris Mitchell when we're talking about phrases sometimes overheard in newsrooms: 'Colin has sent this article which he wants published' or 'Colin won't be happy if you run that story'.

Having worked at News Corp for seventeen years, I know there are only three people who can tell the editors of *The Australian* what they can or can't use: Rupert Murdoch, Lachlan Murdoch and Colin Rubenstein. Only one of them doesn't have Murdoch as his surname. That's power.

~

So those are the techniques used to prevent a free flow of information, but what are the consequences? A major one is that there are several important facts which you will never—or rarely—get from an Australian media outlet. For example, no other country has as many children under military occupation as Israel. Israel blockades most of Gaza's borders, with Egypt controlling the southern border. But leading international law authorities argue that Gaza is in reality occupied. Yoram Dinstein, Israel's leading authority on international law, has aligned himself with the 'prevalent opinion' that the Israeli occupation of Gaza is not over.[12] And Human Rights Watch has stated that, since Israel still preserves near-total dominance of the strip, 'whether the Israeli army is inside Gaza or redeployed around its periphery, it remains in control'.[13]

Israel is also one of the last countries on Earth to maintain a military occupation. Most countries that have been an occupier have found it too difficult and too costly to sustain. The French believed the price they were paying to occupy Algeria was too high. The Syrians found occupying Lebanon too problematic—they couldn't work out who among the Lebanese had power and who didn't. The Indonesians found the price they paid for occupying East Timor was too high in terms of international criticism, particularly from the United States. Yet Israel persists with its occupation, which is maintained by its official army, the Israeli Defense Forces, and its unofficial army, the settlers—many settlements in the West Bank host IDF bases.

And it's a fact that Israeli settler leaders have worked with the army from the early days of the occupation to plan Jewish settlements so as to make a Palestinian state physically impossible. I know this to be so because settler leaders openly admit it, and this is well documented in the archives of Israel. And a final fact: I could have a civilised discussion about these issues with most Israelis, including politicians and army officers, but such a discussion in Australia would be virtually impossible, as it would quickly descend into abuse.

It's not just the power that AIJAC holds but also the hardline positions that it advocates. AIJAC is aligned to the far right of Israeli politics—they may occasionally talk about a two-state solution, but in my view this is purely lip-service. If they genuinely wanted a two-state solution they would push not just for an end to new settlements but for the winding back of existing settlements. AIJAC's far-right position has become more and more obvious. Chris Mitchell, who has dealt with the pro-Israel lobby for decades and visited Israel many times, watched AIJAC radicalise. He tells me: 'I suppose I always took the view that in many ways what happened with AIJAC and other places is that when the neocons really got control of the [George W] Bush administration, you had a real radicalisation of the Israeli lobby here, almost hand in hand.'

That, of itself, is an extraordinary assessment—to have a former editor-in-chief of Rupert Murdoch's flagship, the most pro-Israel newspaper in Australia by the length of a kibbutz, describe Australia's most influential Jewish lobby group as having undergone 'radicalisation'. Mitchell adds that the Israeli–Palestinian situation is 'not so black and white as people like Rubenstein make out'. He says it is 'nonsense' to believe that the next generation of Palestinian children is going to be any less committed to statehood than the current one.

In my assessment, and Chris Mitchell's, the real problem is not Rubenstein and the pro-Israel lobby. They are paid to ensure that, in Australia, Israel is painted in the best possible light—with as few, or preferably no, references to settlements. 'Colin's pushing a position that it's his job to do,' says Mitchell. 'Editors get the freedom that they are strong enough to take. I think part of the problem with editors who allow themselves to be imposed upon by people like Colin is they're not strong-willed.' Mitchell adds: 'It's important for journalists not to have their thought patterns mapped out by lobbyists.'

I've visited the West Bank hundreds of times—both when I lived in Israel and on visits before and after my six years there. I can therefore state with certainty that the picture the lobby in Australia paints for journalists on their fly-in-fly-out, wining-and-dining trips is so far from authentic that it is worse than meaningless. It is damaging because it fills the heads of influential editors with a distorted reality. A large number of the senior editors of Australia's major newspapers have taken those trips. In the interests of full disclosure, I took one in 1997 when I was the editor of *The Sydney Morning Herald*. I can come up with all sorts of rationalisations about why it was worthwhile and how much I learnt. If there was a benefit, it was that when I returned to Jerusalem as a correspondent, I was able to compare what we had been told on that trip with the reality. But I should not have taken the trip—I regret doing so. Now that I know so much more about the subject, I can say that it was wall-to-wall propaganda, choreographed to portray the occupation of the West Bank as normal.

The general line of the trip was that Israel tries so hard to make peace with the Palestinians, and if only the Palestinians were reasonable then there could be a solution. What we were not shown during our six-day trip was that Israel at that very time was encouraging thousands of settlers to move into the West Bank and establish homes on what was often private Palestinian land. On that trip we did not see the army or police demolishing Palestinian houses or helping settlers to move into Palestinian houses. And we heard not a word about the 101 different permits that control the lives of Palestinians—there are permits to go to work, permits to go to a funeral, permits to go to a wedding, even permits to live in your own house.[14] The permit system devised by the Israeli army has turned the lives of Palestinians into a tyranny of bureaucracy and restriction. Meanwhile, the Jewish settlers who may live nearby do not require a single permit and are protected by Israeli civil law.

~

In my view, there is no doubt that self-censorship is occurring in the Australian media when it comes to Israel. Hamish McDonald, who has worked for *The Saturday Paper* and as Asia-Pacific editor of *SMH*, says that in general Australian editors are 'timid' when it comes to Israel: 'The last thing any editor wants is to be described as anti-Semitic. There is a great fear that something you say will be twisted into hostility to Jews.' This fear, says McDonald, leads to 'pre-emptive buckling and a degree of self-censorship'.

The famous Israeli journalist of French origin Charles Enderlin, who endured years of fighting a defamation case against a Jewish–French politician who'd accused Enderlin of fabricating a Gaza story—a fight he finally won[15]—told me that so intimidated was the French media by the pro-Israel lobby that there was no way that the *Four Corners* program I did, 'Stone Cold Justice', would be broadcast in France. He was quickly proven right. After *Four Corners* broadcast the story, *Envoyé Special*, the leading investigative television program at France 2, contacted my wife, Sylvie, a French-Mauritian who had co-produced the *Four Corners* program, to see if she would work on a similar story for French TV. She began arranging interviews and logistics, but the day before the French crew was due to arrive, the producers cancelled, saying that 'the trouble this will cause is not worth it'. So just as *SMH* readers were denied Ed O'Loughlin's farewell feature (an incident I discuss later in this book), French viewers were denied a perfectly legitimate story which, if it had been about Indigenous children in Australia, would have been produced without question. This is self-censorship, the worst censorship of all—it leaves no fingerprints.

I find it disturbing that the claim of anti-Semitism is frequently made against critical reporting of Israel. I remember how Yigal Palmor, a spokesman for Israel, once told me that it did not help Israel for the term 'anti-Semitic' to be used about legitimate journalism. The reason for this is that when there is genuine anti-Semitism, people may no longer pay attention—the boy who cried wolf. In fact, Palmor defended my *Four Corners* report on the Palestinian children. Over lunch one day, he told me: 'Military courts are to justice what military bands are to music ... those children's courts are a stain on our country.'

Yet that term was used by my own colleague at *The Australian*, Greg Sheridan. Under the headline 'Evil and Deeply Untrue', Sheridan urged people to go to the website of AIJAC to see a rebuttal of my *Four Corners* program. I found it staggering that a journalist would be referring people to a privately funded lobby group to debunk a story by one of his colleagues, about whom he said—in the same article—he had 'the greatest respect for'. Sheridan wrote:

> We are living in a time of infamous lies against the state of Israel and the Jewish people. We are witnessing, even in Australia, a recrudescence of some of the oldest types of anti-Semitism. One of the worst recent examples of anti-Israel propaganda that led directly to anti-Semitic outbursts was the *Four Corners* episode 'Stone Cold Justice', purporting to be about Israeli treatment of Palestinian children in the West Bank.[16]

Sheridan wrote that, soon after the program went to air, he attended a Catholic mass in a suburban church. The priest was preaching about forgiveness and he took an example from the Middle East that concerned a heroic

Palestinian whose family had been killed by Israel but who still had 'the moral grandeur' to forgive the Israelis. The priest, wrote Sheridan, said nothing else about the Middle East, about all the malevolence and genuine evil there—the only thing the priest thought worth mentioning was a generic Israeli crime. Sheridan added: 'With 2000 years of Christian anti-Semitism behind him, the priest had no hesitation in presenting Israel as the killer of innocent families and the only question in the Middle East being one of the moral greatness of the Palestinians in forgiving the Israelis.'

How bizarre is that? The Israeli spokesman in Jerusalem told me it was legitimate journalism, yet my own foreign editor in Melbourne invoked anti-Semitism. To begin with, the story wasn't about 'the Jewish people'. It was about a policy of the Israeli Government that supports having two different legal systems apply to two different ethnic groups in the same geographical area.[17] That is factual. Israeli media themselves have done that same story. And, after my story, Israel itself conceded the law was bad and needed to be reviewed.

It was not even clear that the priest had seen the *Four Corners* program! But because he gave one example of a Palestinian man who had forgiven those who had killed his family, he was suddenly lumbered with '2000 years of Christian anti-Semitism behind him'. This sort of reaction means that a genuine, fact-based discussion about the nature of Israel's occupation of the West Bank—and whether it should be permanent—is made more difficult. It is my view that branding reporting or discussion about Israel as anti-Semitic can have the effect of closing down genuine debate.

Sheridan used the allegation again in June 2021 upon the departure of Benjamin Netanyahu, who had been widely criticised around the world and inside Israel. Sheridan saw anti-Semitism rearing its head once more. Indeed, it was a 'recrudescence'—yet again. He wrote:

> The apparent end of Benjamin Netanyahu's 12-year reign as Prime Minister of Israel is a grand historical moment. So, sadly, is the recrudescence of one of the most putrid hatreds in history, the renewed rise of anti-Semitism. Are these two connected? Yes they are. Let me be absolutely clear. 'Bibi' Netanyahu did not cause, and does not bear responsibility for, any speck of anti-Semitism. But the prolonged demonisation of Netanyahu is itself an element, and an enabler, of the new, foul, racist hatred of Jews, especially evident in the West.[18]

Again, just as I could not see how a story about Israel's military court system was an attack on Jews around the world, I cannot see how criticism of Netanyahu—who Sheridan himself said in the same article 'has demonised his domestic opponents, casting them as a grave threat to Israeli security and thus undermining the credibility of national security language'—can in any way be an enabler of 'foul, racist hatred of Jews'. In fact, when I lived in Israel, there were no greater demonisers of Netanyahu than a large section of the Israeli public and their media. Were those Israelis and newspapers anti-Semitic?

~

One of the most frequently used weapons of the pro-Israel lobby is its determination to never give up. Journalists and editors across Australia know that if you write anything critical of Israel—or favourable towards Palestinians—you open up not just a Pandora's box but a seemingly depthless one.

My own organisation, the ABC, has seen many examples of this. A notable one occurred in late 2020 after the Melbourne-based Australian Palestinian writer Samah Sabawi submitted an article to the ABC's Religion & Ethics department. Without telling Sabawi, Scott Stephens from that department sent the opinion piece to Bren Carlill at the Zionist Federation of Australia. Stephens then sent an email to Sabawi which contained words similar to those which Carlill would later use in criticising Sabawi's article. Stephens told Sabawi: 'But no Israeli plan has actually been tabled … all of this is also conjecture.' In an article which Stephens ran alongside Sabawi's, Carlill wrote: 'Given that no-one has seen any plan, all this is conjecture.'

Stephens later told an internal ABC inquiry that he had sent these words to Sabawi 'not to censure' but to 'pre-empt a certain line of criticism'. Sabawi complained that her article had been sent to the Zionist Federation without her approval and that the ABC had allowed a 'companion piece' to be posted at the same time attacking her piece point by point—that the Zionist Federation had had the advantage of seeing it well before it was published. An investigation by the ABC's Audience and Consumer Affairs team found that Stephens had breached the organisation's principles and that Sabawi should have been advised before her work was sent to Carlill. Audience and Consumer Affairs told Sabawi:

Had you been advised that this approach was to be taken, not only would you have had the opportunity to query it, but also any *appearance* that the ABC's editorial processes had been outsourced to a lobby group would have been avoided. This finding is also informed by the highly contested and adversarial nature of the issues to hand, and the strong criticisms made of your article by Dr Carlill. The ABC apologies for this lapse, and as a result of your complaint, the Religion and Ethics team will produce an information fact sheet for contributors, and I understand that your complaint and this finding has been discussed with Scott Stephens.[19]

While that issue raised concerns, a later email probably has greater implications for coverage of the issue. On 9 September 2020, Stephens wrote to a potential contributor saying that he had been caught in 'a seemingly never-ending cross-fire of complaint and counter-complaint, after Abu Sitta's piece earlier this year and Samah Sabawi's piece more recently, and then responses to both by Bren Carlill'. It was what Stephens said next that, in my view, sends alarm signals: 'The Israel/Palestine matter has been "too hot" and we've made an editorial decision to "go quiet" on the matter for a while. It's been immensely time-consuming and personally exhausting/bruising. I'll let you know when we might revisit the topic. Best, Scott.'

For me, this could be seen as a justification for creating the most possible noise or biggest backlash against articles or viewpoints. The pro-Israel lobby, for example, knows that its complaints often tie up editors and journalists. That's why an organised campaign of complaints to *Four Corners* began several hours before my program was screened in 2014. To have a senior content maker at the ABC say that the issue had become 'too hot' and therefore 'we've made an editorial decision to "go quiet"' is very disturbing. When I asked him about this email, Scott Stephens said he did not wish to discuss 'internal editorial deliberations'.

~

It's the afternoon of 14 March 2017 and a young woman sits at her desk in the Sydney office of *The Australian*. Her name is Jennine Khalik, a 23-year-old Palestinian Australian who joined the paper less than two years earlier. The editor, Clive Mathieson, had—smartly—recruited her because the paper had not a single Arabic speaker, yet there were so many potential stories among Sydney's 400 000-strong Arabic-speaking communities. One of the stories which Khalik researched was the attempts by Islamic State to recruit over the internet young, disenfranchised men in those western Sydney communities to fight in Syria, along with ongoing coverage of the local heightened anti-Muslim attacks against schools and businesses. But it was a story about a Palestinian singer, and the backlash it prompted on that March afternoon, that would change the course of her career.

As a senior reporter on the paper at the time, I saw first-hand the value of Khalik. We worked together on a few stories regarding Sydney's Arab communities, reporting on the burden that elders in those communities carried in trying to stop their sons from being recruited. On one occasion, we went to Punchbowl to research a story on the pressures facing local young men at the peak of the Syrian civil war. We could not have done the story without Khalik's language skills, local knowledge and credibility in those communities. As the editor of *The Sydney Morning Herald* years earlier, I'd sat in countless meetings where people had talked about the need to recruit journalists to reflect a changing Australia. Here we had it at *The Australian*.

Khalik brought to the paper stories from a swathe of Sydney which had been underreported, including ones about Syrian and Iraqi refugees coming to Australia. Most media groups are headquartered in the inner city, and most don't reflect the contemporary demographic. With three million or so people living in western Sydney, this was a part of the country which could put governments into office—John Howard knew that better than most, hence his decision to govern with 'Howard's battlers' front of mind. But life was becoming difficult for Khalik—she'd come to the attention of pro-Israeli groups.

At the end of her first year, at a Christmas barbecue for staff, Clive Mathieson had a frank conversation with Khalik. He told her that Israeli diplomats had come to see him and that she had been 'on the agenda'. Khalik, then only twenty-one, was shocked to discover she was the subject of such high-level discussions. Khalik recalls that Mathieson 'mentioned to me that there were lobby groups who were very upset at the editors for hiring me. But he said he was happy to have hired me and added that it was an asset I was able to speak Arabic.' She adds that while it was advantageous to speak a language other than English, she did not want to be pigeon-holed as a reporter who only did stories about a community she shared a language with: 'It was extremely reductive and I had proven I had the skills to report on any news item. I felt like I had been taken advantage of, and it gave me constant anxiety to be put on stories about an already over-reported, over-policed and disempowered community. The only reason I stayed

was out of [a] sense of stubbornness and resistance—
I knew there were high-level people who wanted me
gone because I was Palestinian, and I thought if I was
at least involved in those community stories, I could …
mitigate the sensationalism and fear-mongering in some
ways, and report on a timely issue with humanity and
three-dimensionality if I was going to stick around while
dealing with pro-Israel lobbyists on my tail. But that
back-fired in its own way.'

Clive Mathieson confirms Khalik's recollection of
the conversation at the barbecue. He says that Israeli
diplomats did come to see him, and that during the
meeting they raised the presence at the paper of Jennine
Khalik. His recollection is that one of them said words to
the effect of: 'It's interesting that you have a Palestinian
activist working on your paper.' They noted Khalik's
social media use. In what Mathieson describes as an
otherwise good-natured meeting, the diplomats made
it clear there was some 'surprise and discomfort' with
the newspaper's decision to employ Khalik. Mathieson
told them he gave Khalik his full support. About that
time, officials at the Israeli Ministry of Foreign Affairs in
Jerusalem began following Khalik on Twitter.

'We recruited Jennine because the paper needed to
have more expertise in diverse communities,' Mathieson
says. 'The idea that in 2015 *The Oz* did not have a single
person on staff who spoke Arabic, who had Chinese
language skills or, to the best of my knowledge, was
Indigenous, was a serious concern. We went out of our

way to try to address that and hiring Jennine was part of that process. The idea that someone cannot write about their own community is ridiculous. For years the paper had James Murray, an Anglican priest, writing about Christianity.'

Early in 2016, Mathieson left the paper. Khalik, meanwhile, continued to be targeted by the pro-Israel lobby. She was also coming under pressure from elements of Sydney's Islamic leadership, including the office of the then mufti. It was clear to the editors and to Khalik herself that the pressure would continue to be intense while she was reporting the sorts of news stories that she was. It was agreed that a stint in the Arts section would be good for her—journalists in Arts tend to come under less scrutiny than when writing for the news pages.

But Khalik's problems did not end with that move. She wrote a story about how the Victorian Education Department was being lobbied to remove from its curriculum a play by Samah Sabawi—a love story set in Gaza. Khalik interviewed Sabawi and wrote about the pressure to remove the play. One Jewish group telephoned the news desk to complain that a journalist of Palestinian heritage was writing a story about a Palestinian playwright. Khalik says the person on the news desk who took the call walked to her desk to tell her about the call: 'I couldn't believe it. Imagine if someone called up saying "How dare you have a Jewish journalist write on this topic."'

Khalik thought about leaving the paper, but she says that while the lobby group wanted to get rid of her, 'I wanted to leave on my own terms.' It was an incident on the afternoon of 14 March 2017 that she says finally did it for her.

Khalik's managers in the Arts section had asked if she would write a story about a visiting Palestinian refugee and singer, Oday al-Khatib, who would be performing in Australia. She duly interviewed al-Khatib, who said: 'I'm so proud that someone from Palestine can represent his people on the world stage.' Khalik wrote up the interview and filed the story. She says it was what happened next that shocked her. One of the paper's sub-editors walked up to her desk and began shouting. Khalik later wrote a private account of what happened:

> He started yelling, while standing over me. 'You used "Palestine" in this piece. PALESTINE DOES NOT EXIST. You have to remove it from the article. How are you a journalist? Palestine is NOT a place. Do I have to teach you how to be a journalist? What kind of journalist are you, using the world Palestine? You're a joke. Am I the one who has to teach you how to be a journalist?'

Khalik says the rest of the conversation was a blur and that the sub finally swore and walked off. 'I sat still for a moment,' she says. 'I stood up, scooped my phone, went to the bathroom and called my mum in tears.' Khalik left the paper soon after—in fact, she has now left journalism, prompting regret for not having finished her law degree, which she abandoned to become a journalist.

One of Khalik's former colleagues at *The Australian*, Gina Rushton, says she watched Khalik's spirit be eroded: 'That place really broke her. I felt very sorry for her because I saw the pressure she was under knowing that people were contacting the editors to complain that she was on the paper.' Rushton says the paper benefited from Khalik's contacts in various Islamic and Arab communities in western Sydney and she gave them a number of exclusive stories they never would have gotten otherwise. 'It felt like they mined her for a lot of these stories and then when she was under pressure they didn't have her back,' Rushton says. 'I saw the difference in treatment between one person in the newsroom who took a paid junket to Israel and could tweet whatever she wanted and Jennine who was basically warned off from tweeting. Her tweets these days are obviously more outspoken as she hasn't been a reporter for a little while, but it feels important to note back then they didn't seem to breach any social media policy or raise questions about bias or anything. After Jennine was yelled at she was not just upset but confused. She told me that he [the sub-editor] kept shouting that Palestine doesn't exist but she said to me that the singer she had just interviewed said he was proud to represent Palestine on the world stage. So her view was what was she to say in the story if that's how he described himself?'

In May 2021, Jennine Khalik organised a petition and an open letter about coverage of the Israeli–Palestinian conflict.[20] The open letter gained more than 700 signatories while the petition took more than 20 000 signatures. Khalik believes her petition has tapped into a growing discontent about how the conflict is being covered: 'I think there was something different about the most recent Gaza war—I think the public is starting to understand that there is something wrong with the way the issue is covered by most Australian media outlets. There's a culture of fear in newsrooms when it comes to Israel. It was horrible going into work every day in constant fear of intimidation. It was traumatising and that's why I got out of newsrooms.'

Hamish McDonald says: 'If you are a journalist in your twenties or thirties, you may worry about upsetting the Israeli lobby as you do not want to lose a position. There are not many other places to work these days.'

It's not just in newsrooms that fear exists. I saw it even among leaders of the Jewish community who did not want to risk being criticised by the powers that be in the pro-Israel lobby. As the correspondent for *The Australian* in Jerusalem, I was in a privileged position, able to learn about the internal dynamics of the Australian Jewish leadership. *The Australian* was their favourite newspaper, and even though they did not like every article that I wrote, they were still keen for engagement. The Melbourne leaders, in my view, were much more entrenched in their support for the expansion of Jewish settlements and opposition to a Palestinian state than their colleagues in Sydney. One of the Melbourne leaders, for example, when I asked did he think Palestinians should have their own state, quipped: 'They've already got their own state—it's called Jordan!'

The Sydney leadership was less hardline. Over dinner, one of them told me he was opposed to the occupation of the West Bank. He said the only way that Israel could live in peace was if it agreed to a Palestinian state, so that Palestinians ruled over themselves, rather than the Israeli army ruling them. When I asked him why he never said that publicly in Australia, his eyes lit up: 'Are you serious? And have the Melbourne guys declare a fatwa against me?'

Another Sydney-based Jewish leader told me that he, too, was opposed to the occupation. He said Jewish texts made it clear that the Jewish people should never rule over another people. He told me he would send me some of these texts. I contacted him a few times asking for them and finally he sent them to me, but he said he could not publicly express his opposition to the occupation for fear of reprisal from other elements of the Jewish community, and he never again mentioned the occupation in any of our future meetings. My impression was that he was uncomfortable that, as a journalist, I knew that a prominent leader of the Jewish community did not share 'the company line' which supported settlements.

The Melbourne lobby—specifically AIJAC—have always played it hard with editors and journalists.

Maher Mughrabi, now features editor at *The Age*, recalls an incident from when he was foreign editor of *The Age* and *SMH*. It was during the 2014 Gaza war. Mark Leibler and Colin Rubenstein walked into *The Age* office to meet the then editor, Andrew Holden. Mughrabi says Holden asked him to sit at a desk nearby 'in case he needed to call me in'. Mughrabi was therefore in a prime position to observe the meeting. 'I watched from the other side of the glass as Mr Leibler shouted and gesticulated while going through a scrapbook of cuttings, at various points turning purple with rage,' Mughrabi recalls. 'Anyone who thinks that such a display by an esteemed member of the Australian community doesn't have a chilling effect is kidding themselves. I have seen its effects in the years since in hesitancy on the part of editors and trepidation about any story which may show Israel in a negative light.'

When I contact Andrew Holden to ask him about the meeting, he tells me it was 'appalling'. He says: 'I got within a split second of ending the meeting and throwing them out of the building because it was outrageous behaviour.' Holden adds that he admired 'the remarkable stoicism' of many Middle East journalists 'despite these attempts to persuade'.

Mughrabi says that the lobbying can verge on the absurd. He points to a controversy in 2019 over the use of the word 'Palestine' as a clue in *The Sydney Morning Herald* crossword. It would seem funny, he says, that such a clue could lead to a controversy were it not for the fact that members of Melbourne's Jewish community publicly said that they had been assured by the newspaper's editors of an 'investigation' into the incident. Under the headline 'Probe into SMH, Age "Palestine" crossword,' *The Australian Jewish News* reported:

> *The Sydney Morning Herald* has launched an investigation after a crossword in its Tuesday edition—also featured in *The Age*—appeared to recognise 'Palestine' as the Holy Land. The issue was first raised by the Australia/Israel and Jewish Affairs Council (AIJAC), which wrote on Facebook, 'Today's crossword clue: The Holy Land. Surely the answer is Israel? Unless, you are doing the crossword in today's Age and Sydney Morning Herald newspapers, where the Holy Land is apparently Palestine.' *SMH* ... told *The AJN*: 'The crosswords are provided by an external contractor [they're not done in-house] so I wasn't aware of this. We are making inquiries about this immediately.' The papers also put out a statement in which they said they 'apologise for any offence caused'. AIJAC executive director Colin Rubenstein told *The AJN* the 'real puzzle' is why 'a wrong or, at best, incomplete answer' has been given.[21]

Even for a clue in a crossword, there needs to be an investigation.

~

A serious reassessment of how the Israeli–Palestinian conflict is being covered is not just happening in Australian media outlets. In the United States in June 2021, an open letter 'written by and for journalists' called on the American media to stop 'obscuring Israeli occupation and the systemic oppression of Palestinians'.[22] It was signed by more than 800 journalists, including from *The Washington Post* and *Los Angeles Times*.

Since the latest Gaza conflict, *The New York Times*, a paper very supportive of Israel and traditionally reluctant to write about life under occupation, has changed tack. On 22 May 2021, it ran a story titled 'Life under Occupation: The Misery at the Heart of the Conflict', which focused on the issue that sparked the war: the attempts to evict six Palestinian families from their homes in the neighbourhood of Sheikh Jarrah in East Jerusalem so that Jewish settlers could move in.[23] It was reported that, for the roughly three million Palestinians living in the West Bank and East Jerusalem, 'the story was exceptional only because it attracted an international spotlight'. The story talked about 'the fragility and cruelty of life under military rule, now in its second half-century'. It told of how in East Jerusalem (which includes part of the Old City of Jerusalem), Palestinians find it nearly impossible to obtain building permits, in contrast to Jews. It reported how Israeli Government officials, influenced by settlers, set about 'clearing' one Palestinian house after another. It quoted an Israeli official saying that the reason for wanting to demolish

Palestinian homes in East Jerusalem was to restore views of the Old City 'as they were in the days of the Bible'. It reported how one Palestinian mother, who tried to rush her daughter to an East Jerusalem hospital after she had accidentally inhaled house-cleaning chemicals, was blocked by Israeli soldiers. It reported that, in 2020, seventy-nine Palestinian homes in East Jerusalem were demolished by their owners—Israeli officials tell Palestinians that they can choose either to demolish their own homes or pay about $10 000 to cover the cost of Israel doing it. A story like this would have been rare in *The New York Times* before the 2021 Gaza conflict.

Another story in *The New York Times*—published two days earlier than 'Life under Occupation'—was headlined 'Israel Is Falling Apart, because the Conflict Controls Us'.[24] It was a guest essay by Dahlia Scheindlin, a policy fellow at the New York–based Century Foundation who has advised eight national election campaigns in Israel. Her central argument was that it was time for the world to accept that it was not just Israel that controlled Palestinians but that 'Palestine also controls Israel'. The occupation, she contended, had permeated every part of Israeli society and community wellbeing. She noted that, since 2009, Israeli governments had passed discriminatory laws which elevated the status of Jews over Palestinians and were tailored to constrain criticism of the occupation. 'Decades of Palestinian suffering should have brought Israel's occupation to an end by now,' she wrote. 'But the folly of territorial conquest and international realpolitik has been stronger.'

Something has changed. It could be that, after the latest Gaza conflict, a paper famous for its support for human rights believes it cannot keep ignoring the Palestinians' situation. I think there are two other factors. The first is the strong emergence of the Black Lives Matter movement, which the *NYT* has supported and which has linked itself to the Palestinian cause. The second is the election of Joe Biden. While Donald Trump supported the far right and its desire to entrench the occupation, President Biden has reintroduced a more orthodox US policy towards Israel: while turning a blind eye to settlements, it is notionally supportive of a two-state solution.

~

It was a comment made by Colin Rubenstein on the steps of the Victorian Parliament in 2014, at the height of the Gaza War—'Israel does more than any other country to avoid killing civilians'—that highlighted to me the disparity between the reality in Israel and what lobbyists try to convince journalists to write. In 2009, during the first Gaza war I covered, I saw from the border the Israeli army drop what looked like cobwebs of white balls onto civilians in Gaza. I spoke to doctors who said people were being brought into hospital with burns which seemed consistent with white phosphorous.

Dropping any chemical weapon is a war crime—in this case, its effect would be particularly damaging given Gaza is one of the most populated places on earth. I telephoned the Israeli army's spokesperson, Avital Leibovich, to put to her that it appeared Israel had used white phosphorous. She was outraged: 'How dare you accuse us of doing something like that! It's offensive and outrageous that you would buy that sort of propaganda.' At the time, to fend off questions from the foreign media, the IDF set up an inquiry. Several months later, when the world media had moved on, it released its report. Israel admitted that it had used white phosphorous on Gaza—in 'limited quantities'.[25]

Soon after my arrival in Jerusalem, I was invited to lunch by an Israeli whose job was to lobby foreign journalists for positive stories about Israel. 'I noticed that you've used the word "occupied" and reported negative stories about the Israeli army,' he said. 'Do you realise the Israeli army, by any measure, is the most moral army in the world?' I replied that while I was not uncritical of the Australian armed forces, I couldn't see why the Israeli army was more moral than the Australian army. 'We are,' he said. 'The longer you live here, the more you will realise that.' When I asked why, he replied: 'Because the Israeli Army has Jewish values.'

What could I say to that? I replied: 'So what if there are two Australian soldiers in a trench in Tarin Kowt fighting the Taliban and one is Jewish and one is not? Is one of those soldiers more moral than the other?'

He looked at me and smiled—and said he did not think we would agree on this subject.

That view of the superiority of the Israeli army over all others is not peculiar to Israelis. On the steps of the Victorian Parliament, Rubenstein had said that a foreign army conducted itself with higher moral standards than the army of the country of which he was a citizen. I cannot count the number of times both Israelis and leaders of Australia's Jewish community have echoed the same view.

~

For the six years I was based in Jerusalem, I was able to report exactly what I saw. This was only possible because of the support of *The Australian* editors at the time: Chris Mitchell, Paul Whittaker and Clive Mathieson.

I have no doubt that, had Chris Mitchell not pushed back against Rubenstein and the lobby, I would not have survived that long in the posting. An example of how Mitchell had stood up to Rubenstein came one day during a phone call when Rubenstein made an observation about Elisabeth Wynhausen, a Jewish writer on the paper who many years earlier had written a feature about how the pro-Israel lobby tries to stifle journalists. According to Mitchell, Rubenstein described Wynhausen as 'a self-loathing Jew'. Mitchell tells me: 'I thought it was inappropriate for him to be making that kind of comment about one of my staff.

For some time after that I stopped taking his calls.'
Mitchell says that, as a result, Rubenstein instead began
calling Nick Cater.[26] (Colin Rubenstein has said he
does not recall calling Wynhausen a 'self-loathing Jew',
that that did not sound like the kind of terminology he
would use.)

I wrote to Mitchell from Jerusalem to say that
I thought AIJAC had become arrogant about its
influence on the paper. I had written a story for *The
Weekend Australian Magazine* about a Palestinian
whose house in the Old City had been taken over by
armed Jewish settlers when he had moved out to have
the house renovated. At that time, Steve Waterson
was the editor of the magazine, and he told me that
Cater had dropped by his office a few days before publication of my piece and said: 'If there's one mistake
in this article, Colin will come down on us like a ton
of bricks.'

Upon my return to Australia, I interviewed Mitchell
for *Balcony over Jerusalem*. He told me:

Most of the attacks on you came from Colin Rubenstein
and Bob Magid [the owner of *Australian Jewish News*].
The stories you did on Palestinian children were the
ones that most upset Colin Rubenstein. My view was
that in an elected democracy on the other side of
the world we should be able to openly and honestly
canvass an issue like this without the interference from
a lobby group in Melbourne.[27]

While Mitchell, Whittaker and Mathieson backed me when attacks from the lobby occurred, Cater was the one editor with whom I had problems. On one occasion, he invited an official from the Israeli Embassy in Canberra into the Sydney office. As she was taken to meet editors of the various sections of the paper, she promptly proceeded to criticise my work. When I woke up in Jerusalem to find emails from colleagues telling me about what the official had been doing, I wrote to Mitchell: 'Chris, do you realise that while I was asleep an official from a foreign government has been wandering the floor of our head office bagging me?' Mitchell had not known, and he was furious. He said he would be telling Cater as much in no uncertain terms.

It got to the point where a couple of times on a Friday, when I had a story that was critical of Israel, the foreign news desk and I agreed that the story would not be mentioned in the morning conference. Friday was the one day that Cater was in charge of running the editorial conference, as he was the editor of the next day's paper, *The Weekend Australian*. I know that on one occasion, the first that Cater knew that a story critical of Israel was in the paper was when he picked it up at home on a Saturday morning. He complained to Chris Mitchell that the story had been published without him knowing. Mitchell had retorted: 'So Nick, who exactly is the editor of *The Weekend Australian*?' When I ask Mitchell if he knew that on a few occasions we 'hid' some stories from the Friday conference, he replies: 'I was aware that he [Cater] was running interference for the Israelis.' Mitchell says that he had originally decided to post me to Jerusalem as he wanted to expand the paper's coverage of Israel, and he didn't really think it was appropriate for his number three, Cater, to intervene.

Nick Cater did not wish to engage with me for this book. I phoned him to tell him that I wanted to discuss all these issues, and specifically that Mitchell had said he'd 'run interference' both on my role in the Middle East and for Israel. Cater said that discussion of what had happened on a newspaper should be kept in a 'cone of silence' and not be discussed in books. He said he felt Mitchell had revealed too much about his time as an editor in his memoir,[28] and that, likewise, I had revealed too much in my book. When I said that they were no longer internal matters when they involved outside organisations such as the Israeli Embassy or AIJAC, Cater said: 'I've been out of the media for many years and I have absolutely no interest in discussing these issues. Let's just agree to end this conversation in a civilised way.'

While I was having my insider battles, outsiders trying to put forward a Palestinian point of view in *The Australian* were having their own issues. Professor Bassam Dally is one of Australia's most respected academics. He obtained his PhD in combustion science from Sydney University and was head of the School of Mechanical Engineering at the University of Adelaide. He has contributed to many research fields, including aerodynamics and renewable energy, and has published more than ninety papers in international journals. Of Palestinian heritage, Professor Dally used to frequently try to get a Palestinian perspective into Australian newspapers, because, he says, the Palestinian side is rarely given an airing compared with the Israeli side. At the time he was trying to get articles published, he was an executive member of the Australia Palestine Advocacy Network. APAN is an organisation that includes church groups, trade unions, academics and Jewish groups, and which supports a two-state solution—the official position of the Australian, US and UK governments. Dally is anything but a radical, yet he believes he was met with hostility when he tried to have articles published in *The Australian*. For years he has been monitoring pro-Palestinian compared with pro-Israeli articles published in Australian newspapers and says in the best year, five pro-Palestinian pieces were published in *The Australian* compared with 20 pro-Israeli articles. That 'best year', he says, was under Chris Mitchell, who would at least take his phone calls, but he says since Mitchell retired there has been virtually no Palestinian voice in the paper: 'Under Chris Mitchell at least we could from time to time get our point of view printed. Since Mitchell left we've only been able to get one or two articles published over five years.'

Mitchell tells me that he had to push hard for Dally's articles to be published. Again, this is extraordinary—the most senior editor having to push to get an opinion piece in his own newspaper. On one occasion, he says, the editor of the opinion page, Rebecca Weisser, refused to publish a piece submitted by Dally. Mitchell says she was supported in this by Nick Cater. 'He [Cater] came in to defend Rebecca after Rebecca basically said, "I'm not going to do it" [publish the piece]. I said, "Yes you are, and you're going to buy him lunch too!"' Mitchell says, laughing. Weisser reluctantly published the piece—'I'm very strong-willed, you know,' says Mitchell. I rang Weisser to ask why, if Mitchell was correct, the editor-in-chief of *The Australian* would have to push her to run an opinion piece by a moderate, academic Palestinian. 'I have nothing to say on the record or off the record,' she said, before hanging up.

Professor Dally says there is now a strong view among supporters of a two-state solution that being published in News Corp papers is counterproductive. Firstly, the papers allow 'vicious, sometime bordering on defamatory' letters in response, and secondly, the company can use the one or two articles to claim that it covers the Palestinian side. Dally has had email exchanges with Alan Howe, whom he wrote to when Howe was the editor of the opinion page, coming after Rebecca Weisser. In one missive, Howe wrote:

The Palestinian Authority should be ashamed of itself. Rather than send me words like these, why not encourage your countrymen and woman [sic] to lay down their arms? Now there's an idea. And when you do that, please write an opinion about it and I will publish it. Best wishes to you, Alan Howe.

Dally says he felt humiliated on receiving this response, and confirms that a senior editorial executive later rang to apologise. 'This was the opinion page of the national newspaper,' says Dally. 'This was meant to be the page where different points of view were reflected as part of free speech. Yet the hostility of some of the responses I got was disturbing.'

Alan Howe says he does not remember the specific piece that he rejected, but says that 'the Palestinians' cause and needs are acute and they demand honest, alert, fearless and informed spokesmen and women going in to bat for them. There has not been a representative election in either territory for who knows how long? Now *there* is an issue worth an opinion piece. Recycling hate for your neighbours, in my opinion, will not progress the Palestinian cause. Nor will the endless brainwashing of Palestinian children with repugnant lessons in hate.' Howe agrees that Australians do not always get the full picture of the conflict, but he sees it from a different point of view: 'Too often the manipulation of young Palestinians by their elders goes under-reported in Australia, across Europe and the US. And I have taken this issue up face-to-face with the leadership of the Palestinian Authority in Ramallah.'

Some Australian Palestinians raise how, over several years, Howe has been involved with Albert Dadon in organising 'sponsored trips' to Israel by politicians and journalists as part of the Australia Israel Leadership Dialogue. I ask Howe about this, and he tells me that his assistance included providing 'editorial advice' to Dadon and suggesting the names of journalists who should go on these trips; Howe says he was not paid. I ask Howe whether he thinks being involved in these trips compromises his objectivity, or the appearance of objectivity. He replies: 'Being involved in helping with these trips has given me unique access to the Palestinian leadership—and of course Israel's—and the insights that come with that.'

One of the most enthusiastic participants in Dadon's trips is Christopher Pyne, the former federal Liberal Party minister. Pyne tells me that he's been to Israel twelve times, seven or eight with Dadon's dialogue. He says he paid for his own airfares and the dialogue paid for accommodation and transfers in Israel. One year, Dadon helped to arrange for some in his group—including Pyne—to go from Jerusalem to Morocco, his country of birth, to meet its king. When I ask Pyne whether the king paid for his accommodation in Morocco, he says he is not sure: 'I understood the [Dadon] dialogue covered the costs.' In late 2010, Dadon boasted that seventeen members of the House of Representatives and the Senate were going on one of his trips.[29] Put another way, that means that more than 7 per cent of the Australian Parliament was planning to visit Israel on one of the trips organised by Dadon. (Some ultimately withdrew.)

Journalists also joined the trip, including senior political reporters from the ABC, *The Australian Financial Review*, *The Australian*, News Ltd and *The Sydney Morning Herald*.

Four years earlier, Professor Dally was having problems with another newspaper besides *The Australian*. Dally had invited Israeli academic Tanya Reinhart to deliver the annual Edward Said Lecture in Adelaide— Professor Reinhart has written widely on solutions to the Israeli–Palestinian conflict. Professor Dally contacted the main newspaper in Adelaide, *The Advertiser*, to suggest an opinion piece by Professor Reinhart to mark the lecture. The editor did not respond but instead, on the day of the lecture, ran a three-year-old article about female suicide bombers that had appeared in another newspaper—complete with a picture of a Palestinian woman with an explosives vest standing next to her child.[30] 'These sorts of interactions made me feel frustrated, angry and bewildered,' Professor Dally says. 'You feel muzzled, censored and treated with disdain, and it feels like the media is an active participant in the conflict.'

~

To illustrate how divided the Australian media has been on this issue, while the 'Palestinian side' was upset with what it could not get published in *The Australian*, the Israeli Embassy was enraged with what was being published in *The Age*—'by an editor of Palestinian background'.

In 2011, Maher Mughrabi was an editor on the foreign desk at *The Age*. Mughrabi is a journalist of Palestinian heritage, and it was that heritage that the Israeli Embassy targeted on 9 November 2011 when the Israeli ambassador to Australia, Yuval Rotem, wrote to editor-in-chief Paul Ramadge saying that 'under your watch your newspaper allowed the publication by an editor of Palestinian background' of an opinion article the embassy did not like.[31] The ambassador told Ramadge that the views expressed by Mughrabi 'demonstrate that he is unable to maintain the unbiased and impartial posture necessary for the position of foreign news editor'.

For me, it's irrefutable that a double standard exists in that, if someone has a Palestinian or Arab background, they will personally be targeted, whereas this never occurs on the other side. As an exercise, imagine substituting the word 'Palestinian' for 'Jewish'. I doubt that anybody believes the following phrase would ever be uttered by an ambassador: 'Under your watch your newspaper allowed the publication by an editor of Jewish background.' That would—rightly—be shouted down as anti-Semitic. On 22 November, Ramadge wrote to Rotem: 'Mr Mughrabi has been a foreign news editor for several years and there has never been a suggestion that, as a result, our reporting lacked balance … Mr Mughrabi is a highly intelligent, well-informed editor who carries out his responsibilities to the highest journalistic standards. I have full confidence in him.'

A year earlier, supporters of the pro-Israel lobby had been cranking up pressure on *The Age*. At the Fairfax annual general meeting on 10 November 2010, that pressure was applied to the chairman, Roger Corbett.[32] One man told the meeting: 'I am aware of many supporters of Israel who have cancelled their subscriptions, and even advertising, because of your relentless bias against Israel and the general undergraduate style, left-wing nature of much of the foreign coverage and opinion.' Corbett said the man was entitled to his opinion, but it was what he said next that was fascinating. Corbett told the man: 'Only yesterday I was speaking to the Israeli ambassador, and I invited him and he accepted the opportunity of doing an interview with one of our journalists, to put an Israeli point of view if you like.' As a former editor of *The Sydney Morning Herald*, I thought that was a completely inappropriate response. In my opinion, it puts both the editor and the reporter doing the interview in an impossible situation. Interviews and stories should be commissioned on merit, as judged by the editor. What is the editorial merit in this instance? Is the reporter assigned to this being put in a situation where they have to go soft, as it appears it was promised to the ambassador that 'an Israeli point of view' would be put? Why shouldn't every ambassador in Canberra get a free interview? The fact is that a well-managed newspaper should be putting both the Israeli and the Palestinian perspective each time it runs a story involving them.

Supporters of Israel were on a roll at that meeting, with one man saying that Fairfax was 'the most shorted stock' on the exchange, suggesting that people were dumping its shares because of its coverage of Israel. He suggested that the chair sack the editor, the foreign editor and two foreign correspondents. Shareholder activist Stephen Mayne called for calm: 'Media companies need to have free and fair debate. They need to stand by their journalists. They need to listen to critics, and assess whether it's fair, but I think a sweeping attack calling for editors to be sacked, and in such language, I felt, was over the top. I've never heard such language like that on an editorial issue at a media company AGM and I just call for a bit of calm on that sort of language.'

Perhaps Fairfax's most spectacular run-in with the Jewish community came in July 2014 with *The Sydney Morning Herald*'s publication of a cartoon accompanied by a column by Mike Carlton, at the time one of the paper's most read columnists.[33] In an apology ten days later, the *SMH* wrote:

> The cartoon showed an elderly man, with a large nose, sitting alone, with a remote control device in his hand, overseeing explosions in Gaza. The armchair in which he was sitting was emblazoned with the Star of David, and the man was wearing a kippah, a religious skullcap. A strong view was expressed that

the cartoon, by Glen Le Lievre, closely resembled illustrations that had circulated in Nazi Germany. These are menacing cartoons that continue to haunt and traumatise generations of Jewish people.[34]

The words that Carlton wrote in his column were not considered anti-Semitic. In fact, it was a tough critique of the firepower that the Israeli military was using against Gaza. The problem for Carlton came from his responses to some readers, which included calling one reader a 'Jewish bigot'. Carlton argued that he'd 'snapped' after a fortnight of abuse in which he'd been called things like 'you filthy piece of Jew-hating Nazi slime' and told that 'people like you started World War II, Catholic Jew baiter'. Facing possible dismissal, Carlton resigned, tweeting that 'a once great newspaper has buckled to the bullies'.

Darren Goodsir, the *SMH* editor-in-chief from that time, tells me, 'My initial view was that there was nothing too objectionable about the illustration, but over the course of about a week—having spoken with, and taking counsel from, readers, correspondents and senior and junior staff—I reconsidered and apologised about the illustration and the offence it had caused. But not the article itself. In the weeks surrounding this issue, emotions were high, and Mike received a large number of incendiary messages over social media. In time, I became aware that Mike had responded to some of these inflammatory and inappropriate social media messages using extremely offensive language not befitting of an *SMH* staffer or columnist. I spoke with him about this and insisted he apologise to those he had abused, to which he agreed. I felt this was sanction enough, especially given the mitigating circumstances, but the editorial director, Sean Aylmer, felt my actions were not sufficient atonement and contacted Mike to insist he stand aside for a period of time. Mike explained he felt he had already reached an agreement with me and rejected the stand-aside order and resigned … a matter of significant regret for me.'

Asked about his regrets, Goodsir says: 'I think I could have responded with more speed to the legitimate community distress. I also think I could have done more to support Mike given the vitriol he endured from social media correspondents—a phenomenon that sadly has only seemed to get worse since this time.'

Goodsir adds that through this period he experienced a great deal of 'intense lobbying'. From my perspective, the power of the pro-Israel lobby was shown by the agreement that Jewish leaders were able to extract from the paper at the time. Part of that agreement was that Goodsir, his news editors and senior staff attend a seminar about anti-Semitism put on by the NSW Jewish Board of Deputies.

That whole incident highlighted the double standards in the Australian media. Around the same time, *The Australian* ran a cartoon by Bill Leak which was equally confronting for the Palestinian side. It depicted a Hamas

fighter pushing his five-year-old sons into the firing line
with the words, 'There! Now you go out to play and win
the PR war for Daddy.' While Jewish groups were pleased
with their apology from the editors of the *Herald*, there
was no such reality for the editors of *The Australian*.
A spokesperson for the Australia Palestine Advocacy
Network, Issa Shaweesh, condemned the Le Lievre
cartoon, saying it was indefensible and did not represent
Australian Palestinians. He was also appalled by the Leak
caricature, telling *Media Watch*: 'For Palestinians, it's bad
enough that our children are killed in their homes, while
sheltering in UN schools and playing on the beach, but
can you imagine how it feels to be portrayed as sending
them out in the hope that they'll be killed? This is not
only racist and offensive but totally untrue.' Bill Leak told
Media Watch it was 'a well established fact that Hamas
has been stashing weapons in schools while knowing full
well this would turn those buildings, along with their
occupants, into targets for Israeli attacks'.

While that was a debate about what was published,
The Sydney Morning Herald would find itself at the centre
of a controversy about what it did not publish. In May
2008, the Jerusalem-based correspondent of *The Sydney
Morning Herald* and *The Age*, Ed O'Loughlin, filed a
farewell feature reflecting on his five-year posting.[35]
The Age ran the story; the *Herald* spiked it. O'Loughlin
had been the target of much criticism by Jewish groups,
but generally the *SMH* had supported him. O'Loughlin
told *Media Watch* at the time: 'There has been an

intensive lobbying effort to skew the *Herald* and *The Age* to a pro-Israeli position and I've had nothing but support until now. That's why I'm surprised that they pulled my final piece.' What those *Herald* readers could not read, for example, was O'Loughlin's assessment that the Israeli army had a 'culture of denial and impunity, repeatedly condemned by Israeli and foreign (human) rights groups'. Or that for Palestinians, their confidence was not high 'when you have reason to fear that someone you can't see is studying you on a computer screen, or through a gun sight'. That sort of reporting is carried almost daily in Israel. Yet readers in Australia were denied those words. And it certainly wasn't because O'Loughlin couldn't write—the following year he was long-listed for the Man Booker Prize.

So why did these words never appear in *The Sydney Morning Herald*? O'Loughlin himself says he was told 'informally' that there were concerns about how the pro-Israel lobby would react to it. The editor who decided not to publish it was Alan Oakley, who discussed the piece with senior journalist Hamish McDonald. McDonald tells me that he recalls Oakley saying to him at the time that 'he was going to a Jewish Board of Deputies' dinner a couple of weeks later and couldn't face the grilling he would get if he ran it'. I ring Oakley to ask him why the story did not run and to put to him Hamish McDonald's recollection. 'Hamish has probably got a better memory than me,' he says, adding that he definitely would have discussed the story with others.

After I phone Oakley, he re-reads the story and calls me back: 'I would make the same decision today not to publish. I thought for a reflection of Ed's time covering the conflict it was a one-sided view—the Palestinian view.'

~

While News Corp papers do not try to hide their support for Israel, some media outlets believe the Israeli–Palestinian conflict is given too much attention. Schwartz Media is the most notable of these. Founded by Melbourne-based property developer Morry Schwartz, the group publishes *The Saturday Paper*, *The Monthly*, *Quarterly Essay*, Black Inc. books and *Australian Foreign Affairs*—not mass-circulation publications but influential ones. Schwartz Media's coverage of Israel has seen a social media campaign launched against it, which Morry Schwartz believes is motivated by anti-Semitism: 'The campaign is like information terrorism. We're being targeted by an extremely savage social media campaign. And you know why this is happening? In my view it's because I am Jewish. In my view this is anti-Semitism. I'm from a Holocaust family, and I know what anti-Semitism feels like.'

In 2014, Schwartz launched *The Saturday Paper*. It would target a left-of-centre inner-city readership. The person hand-picked to be its editor, Erik Jensen, contacted Hamish McDonald and said he would like McDonald to be the publication's world editor.

McDonald said yes. But then, McDonald recalls, Jensen said 'something like "There's one touchy subject—Morry [Schwartz] is very sensitive about stories about Israel. He would not like to see Israel under attack."'

It's worth reflecting on that conversation—here were two journalists as far away as it's physically possible to be from Israel and the recruiting editor is telling the would-be world editor that Israel is a 'touchy' subject. The problem with conversations such as these is that there can be a knock-on effect—the word gets out. Whether intended or not, the impact of these discussions can be that if you want to succeed in that organisation, the best thing you can do is avoid this 'touchy' subject. It can lead to self-censorship.

Erik Jensen, when I put to him McDonald's recollection of the conversation, says: 'I shared with him the proprietor's personal view on how the media covers Israel and Palestine. I did this for context. We had both worked together at the *Herald*, and I was sharing an insight into the thinking of our new proprietor. It was by no means a directive about coverage. I don't believe Hamish interpreted it to be. When there was a flare-up a few months later, Hamish led his column with it. He noted the asymmetry of casualties and warned against emboldening "the right-wingers and hard-liners who dominate the Israel lobbies here and in the US". He continued to cover the issue in his time as world editor. Certainly, I don't think he shied from criticising Israel.'

And Morry Schwartz, when I tell him of McDonald's recollection, says: 'What this is probably referring to is that when I started *The Saturday Paper* I told staff I did not want Israel to be over-covered. My view to staff was that I wanted a balance in the coverage of Israel. I don't think Israel needs to be in the paper week after week. But I am a publisher and when there is big news it should be covered, which we showed in the recent Gaza conflict.'

Soon after McDonald took up his new role, the 2014 Gaza war began. He covered it in a factual way each week on the 'World' page, in 300-word updates. But the war was not given prominence. Maddison Connaughton, who took over as editor of *The Saturday Paper* when Jensen was promoted, signed the May 2021 petition circulated by Jennine Khalik—a remarkable situation given that Schwartz Media was one of the outlets which had not been covering Gaza with any rigour. Four weeks after signing that petition, Connaughton surprised her colleagues by resigning. Asked if there was any connection between the two events, Morry Schwartz says: 'As far as I'm concerned there is no connection. I had no problem with her signing that petition—Osman [Faruqi] signed it and he's still working with us.' Asked why Connaughton resigned, Schwartz says: 'I have my hunches, but in truth, I don't know why she resigned.' Likewise, Erik Jensen insists that there was no connection. 'In fact, she asked me about signing the petition and I encouraged her to sign it,' he says. As for Connaughton herself, she tells me, 'At this point in time, I'd prefer not to comment.'

The petition said:

As journalists, reporters and other media workers, we know that the media can do better. Many of us are seeking change but lack sufficient power in our organisations to push back against the status quo. We believe that the coverage of Palestine must be improved, that it should no longer prioritise the same discredited spokespeople and tired narratives and that new voices are urgently needed.[36]

It called on editors to 'consciously and deliberately make space for Palestinian perspectives, prioritising the voices of those most affected by the violence; avoid the "both siderism" that equates the victims of a military occupation with its instigators ...'

During the 2021 Gaza conflict, former morning editor of *The Saturday Paper* Alex McKinnon wrote to his former editors:

While I was at Schwartz, there was an unofficial but widely known editorial policy of avoiding coverage of Israel and Palestine, especially any coverage that could be perceived as being critical of the Israeli government's ongoing human rights abuses of Palestinians. Numerous members of staff mentioned this unspoken policy in conversations with me, unprompted, while I worked there. Many expressed discomfort with it, but all seemed resigned to it.

It was understood that the owner of Schwartz Media, Morry Schwartz, would not allow any Schwartz Media publication to report on Israel or Palestine in a substantive way. While Mr Schwartz's personal views on the subject are his own, it was widely held within the organisation that those views were setting the editorial line for Schwartz Media publications and reporting. While this unofficial policy is widely known within the organisation, and in media circles more broadly, most of Schwartz Media's readership and the general public would be unaware of it. As I said, it is not official. It is not written anywhere. But it is undeniably real. It is a policy of silence.

'I dispute that we have a policy of silence,' says Morry Schwartz. 'I'm not directing this at Alex, but at all journalists and all media outlets. I've found over the years that too often journalists' biases insidiously infect their news reporting and their news analysis. And this has always been particularly egregious in the reporting of the Israeli–Palestinian conflict. They should not be allowing their knee-jerk certainties to surface—neither those with anti-Palestinian sentiments, nor anti-Israeli.'

Alex McKinnon's letter said that, as an organisation that presented itself to its audience as a publisher of fearless and truth-based journalism,

it is dishonest and hypocritical for Schwartz Media to deny its readers coverage of an issue of public importance, and not to explain why. Allowing coverage of any issue to be dictated by the personal views of the company's owner is an unacceptable breach of basic editorial standards. I regret not having formally raised my concerns before today. As I expect many journalists and editors feel—both inside and outside Schwartz Media—I was anxious that doing so would jeopardise my chances of ongoing freelance work, or of potential future employment.

Just as Hamish McDonald had had an interesting conversation with Erik Jensen—the 'touchy' conversation—so had Alex McKinnon had a similar conversation. A journalist who had just joined *The Saturday Paper*—whom McKinnon prefers I not name—wanted to talk to him about the paper. It was an uneventful conversation until the new staff member indicated there was something in particular she wanted to discuss. McKinnon recalls her saying, 'So …' and pausing. 'I knew exactly what she wanted to talk about,' McKinnon recounts. He immediately replied: 'Israel and Palestine?' 'Yes,' she answered. McKinnon says he responded with: 'No-one's directly said to me I can't write about this but they haven't had to because I already knew.' McKinnon tells me: 'But we both kind of agreed that there wasn't much we could do as relatively junior journalists working in an industry where there were relatively few jobs and it was hard to make a future for yourself.'

Alex McKinnon says he believes that, in an ideal world, Morry Schwartz would want a stable of writers who were strongly Zionist, but that he knows this would not be possible while running a left-of-centre newspaper. Therefore, says McKinnon, 'the compromise is that when you work there you don't talk about it and you don't cover it'. They run a few articles, he says, so they can say they do in fact cover Gaza. But, he says, the reality is beginning to hurt—some writers he knows are saying they don't want to write for the group because of its effective non-coverage of Israel and the Palestinians. 'And,' he adds, 'they're deceiving their readership by pretending that they don't have a stance, but they do.'

'How would he know what I would prefer in an ideal world?' responds Morry Schwartz. 'Might be worth taking a quick look at my "stable of writers", a very large number of talented people across all of our titles, and come to your own conclusions.' Schwartz adds: 'I categorically deny Alex's preposterous allegations. I need to do this to protect my reputation, and my 48-year career in publishing.'

Erik Jensen also rejects any suggestion that the Schwartz Media writer group effectively ignores the Israeli–Palestinian conflict: 'This is simply not true. We covered the recent flare-up almost every day in our morning newsletter, *Post*, and in the headlines of our daily news podcast, *7am*. In the first week, it was the only story on our world page—covered in four parts. The following week, we ran a major piece off page one, by

Gregg Carlstrom, detailing the conditions in Gaza. It was also a full episode of *7am* that week, made with our world editor and with Maha Hussaini, a local journalist based in Gaza. The coverage was detailed, fair and rigorous.'

Jensen says, nonetheless, that *The Saturday Paper* was always intended to be Australia-focused. 'When I launched the paper, I saw it as a corrective to holes that existed in the coverage of Australia and Australian politics,' he says. 'I wanted to read longer pieces on issues that were going unreported. The model was *The National Times*. I wanted to put refugee policy on page one and to cover climate policy in more detail. Canberra would be the core of what we would do.'

Writer Omar Sakr also challenged Schwartz editors about the 2021 Gaza conflict. 'When I wrote to the editors of *The Saturday Paper* about their lack of coverage of the ongoing crisis in Gaza, and the absence of Palestinian writers in their publications, I got a generic and utterly unsatisfactory response,' he tells me. 'These days there are so few publications that pay serious writers well, which is why I think not many people have said any-thing. *The Saturday Paper* is a progressive newspaper on every issue except this one. There comes a point where people have to have some integrity and push back. I think the editors should heed their own advertising and take a stand by sitting down—resign. I certainly won't be writing for them again.'

Sakr believes the time has come for the media group to be open about its attitude to covering anything relating to Israelis and Palestinians: 'Schwartz Media claims to offer "a nuanced examination of Australia and the world … providing writing that makes difficult topics clear"—and maybe this would be true, if not for the glaring exception of Palestine and Israel, even when they are the focus of world news. This absence, this refusal, is insidious in its implication that the issue is not worth covering seriously.'

Responds Erik Jensen: 'I admire Alex and Omar enormously. The truth is, there is no directive against covering the Middle East. It's not borne out in our coverage. It's not something that has been told to staff.'

Barrister Greg Barns recently asked on social media: 'So which Palestinian writers have you published and has there been any criticism of #Israel in a Quarterly Essay or @SatPaper.' When I ask Morry Schwartz this question, he replies: 'This is not something I have kept track of. There's certainly never been a direction of any kind not to publish Palestinian writers, or any other writers.' He adds: 'What I would like to say is that the Australian media would be much poorer were it not for us. All I want is balance in everything, including Israel. There has been no direction to my staff. The only thing I have said is that there should not be over-coverage. By balance I mean it is not over-reported compared to other countries. I want the same level of reporting as Poland or Russia or Saudi Arabia or Chechnya.'

～

I'd been in Jerusalem about three years when I was invited to a function for foreign journalists. I found myself in conversation with a senior officer of the Israeli army, born in Australia but having moved to Israel. He'd made 'Aliyah', which means 'rising' to a new life in Israel. The officer knew Australia and its Jewish community well, having grown up in it. As I wrote in *Balcony over Jerusalem*, I told him that, as a journalist, part of my challenge was dealing with the pro-Israel lobby. He laughed. But it was what he said next that I found fascinating. He said he believed that it could be argued that the lobby in Australia had more influence in its country 'pound for pound' than any other. 'The Israel lobby in Australia is the most powerful lobby in the world in terms of [the] impact it has within its own country,' he said. He then outlined his logic for this: Australia had the highest number of Holocaust survivors per capita outside Israel, which helped shape the hardline view of the lobby. Given Australia was a small Jewish community—only about 100 000 people—it was easier to be more united. In Australia there were not the challenges to the powers that be in Melbourne that there were in countries like the United States, where groups such as J Street were diluting the influence of the American Israel Public Affairs Committee (the local equivalent to AIJAC). Several of the wealthiest men in Australia were Jewish and donated significant amounts of money to supporting Israel, particularly the Likud party. And, finally, Australia's Jewish community was much more strongly

Zionist than that in the United States—the percentage of Jews marrying non-Jews in Australia was lower than in America, and about 70 per cent of Jewish Australian adults had visited Israel—a much higher proportion than in the United States or any other countries.

One of the leaders of the Australian Jewish community, Dr Ron Weiser, estimated in 2016 that approximately 10 per cent of the community had made Aliyah and moved to Israel, while many others travelled there regularly. 'The Australian Jewish community is one of the most pro-Zionist and Israel-connected in the world,' he said in an interview.[37]

An example of the glaring double standards that apply in the reporting of Israel is the coverage of an April 2021 Human Rights Watch report on Israel. HRW is not a radical organisation—it's a well-funded, centrist human rights group. In fact, it has been the reporting and analysis of HRW that has allowed media organisations around the world to report on China's human rights atrocities against the Uighur people in the Xinjiang autonomous region. But when it comes to HRW's reporting on Israel, it's a different matter. Many media outlets—including my own organisation, the ABC—largely ignored HRW's landmark report 'A Threshold Crossed: Israeli Authorities and the Crimes of Apartheid and Persecution'. Again, HRW is hardly an anti-Jewish organisation—it is run by Kenneth Roth, the son of a Jewish refugee from Nazi Germany. And HRW's assessment that Israel has now crossed the threshold into an apartheid state—that the deprivations of the Palestinian population are so severe that they amount to the crimes against humanity of apartheid and persecution—is also supported by Israel's own human rights group, B'Tselem. It's important to note that when HRW and B'Tselem assert that Israel has become an apartheid state, they are counting the Jewish and Palestinian populations of Israel and the West Bank and the Palestinian population of Gaza.

On releasing the HRW report, Kenneth Roth said that Israel's rule was more than 'an abusive occupation': 'These policies, which grant Jewish Israelis the same rights and privileges wherever they live and discriminate against Palestinians to varying degrees wherever they live, reflect a policy to privilege one people at the expense of another.'[38] The report itself said:

> Laws, policies and statements by leading Israeli officials make plain that the objective of maintaining Jewish Israeli control over demographics, political power and land has long guided government policy. In pursuit of this goal, authorities have dispossessed, confined, forcibly separated and subjugated Palestinians by virtue of their identity to varying degrees of intensity. In certain areas … these deprivations are so severe that they amount to the crimes against humanity of apartheid and persecution.[39]

The ABC had previously issued a guideline on the use of the word 'apartheid', about which there was some misreporting. It did not ban 'apartheid' from ABC reports. If someone the ABC interviews says that Israel has become an apartheid state, that can be reported. Hence, this was not the reason for the ABC's apparent reluctance to report on 'A Threshold Crossed'.

The HRW report stated:

> The Apartheid Convention defines the crime against humanity of apartheid as 'inhuman acts committed for the purpose of establishing and maintaining domination by one racial group of persons over any other racial group of persons and systematically oppressing them.' The Rome Statute of the International Criminal Court adopts a similar definition: 'inhumane acts … committed in the context of an institutionalized regime of systematic oppression and domination by one racial group over any other racial group or groups and committed with the intention of maintaining that regime.'[40]

One consequence of the sugar-coating of the Israeli–Palestinian issue is that Australians have very little knowledge of the reality of the West Bank. As an Australian journalist, you will be attacked simply for using the word 'occupation'. Yet even the Israeli army accepts that they are occupying Israel.

One of the strangest experiences I had in Israel occurred soon after I arrived there at the start of my six-year correspondent stint. I'll never forget sitting in an

Israeli army base in the West Bank talking to lieutenant colonel Eliezer Toledano, the army's operations officer in the territory. For years in Australia, reading the AIJAC website, I had digested the view that the word 'occupation' was a questionable one in relation to Israel and the Palestinian Territories. I explained this to Toledano and asked him what he thought about it. He looked at me as if I was from another planet. 'I don't know what you're asking,' he replied. 'If this is not occupied then the media has missed one of the biggest stories of our time—withdrawal from the West Bank!' It was such an absurd notion that this hard man of the Israeli army was joking about it.

That meeting with Toledano prepared me for a meeting with a leader of the Melbourne Jewish community. As the correspondent in Jerusalem for *The Australian*, many such leaders would seek me out when they came to the city. Over coffee with one of them, I thought I'd try to have a detailed discussion about the occupation. Israel was taking big hits internationally at the time—not in Australia, of course—paying, in my view, a significant cost in terms of its reputation. So I asked: 'Do you think that Israel is paying too high a cost for its occupation?' He said: 'I don't accept that word'—referring to 'occupation'. I replied that Toledano had used that word, and surely the head of the Israeli army in the West Bank should know the right word to use. 'Toledano is wrong,' he replied. I realised we were not going to have a very deep discussion about possible solutions to the issue.

A year or so later, the same leader returned. Shortly before I met him again, I went to a briefing with Yuval Diskin, the head of Israel's security organisation, Shin Bet (the equivalent of the Australian Security Intelligence Organisation). The first thing Diskin told me was that Shin Bet knew who the extremist Jewish settlers were in the West Bank who were committing acts of violence against Palestinians. 'Why aren't they arrested?' I asked. That was a good question for the government, he said. Shin Bet usually left arrests to the police or army rather than do them itself. The second thing Diskin said was that the current Palestinian Authority leadership—Mahmoud Abbas and Salam Fayyad—was the best that he could remember. He described how previous leader Yasser Arafat had spoken with 'a forked tongue'—saying one thing in English and another in Arabic. But these two leaders, he said, were the best that Israel had had to work with in decades. When I repeated this to the visiting Melbourne Jewish leader, he instantly replied, 'Yuval Diskin is wrong.' This leader maintained he knew more about the reality of the West Bank than one of the most senior Israeli soldiers as well as the head of Israel's domestic intelligence service.

The controlling faction of the Australian Jewish leadership is way out of kilter with security and military experts in Israel. Not long after the Australian Jewish leader asserted that the head of Shin Bet was wrong in his assessment of the willingness of Palestinians to make a peace deal, 106 senior security figures signed a letter urging the Israeli Government to look for a political solution to the conflict. The signatories included two former heads of Mossad and 101 Israeli army veterans with the rank of brigadier or major-general. One of those, retired major-general Eyal Ben-Reuven, said at the time:

> We're on a steep slope toward an increasingly polarised society and moral decline, due to the need to keep millions of people under occupation on claims that are presented as security-related. I have no doubt that the Prime Minister [Netanyahu] seeks Israel's welfare, but I think he suffers from some sort of political blindness that drives him to scare himself and us.[41]

I came to the conclusion that it didn't matter what some of the visiting Jewish leaders heard when they visited Israel. They would never change their view: the Palestinians were not partners for peace and Israel's occupation should continue.

∼

A key weapon of any battle is language. Words are everything. The pro-Israel lobby has even developed a special dictionary to coach its supporters. Called the *Global Language Dictionary*, it was funded by The Israel

Project to guide politicians and journalists on the language to use to win support for settlement expansion:

> The settlements are the single toughest issue for Israel and the hostility towards them and towards Israeli policy that appears to encourage settlement activity is clearly evident. Unless and until Israeli government policy changes, here's the best communication approach ... public opinion is hostile to the settlements—even among supporters of Israel. But if you make the issue part of the larger conversation about finding a way for two peoples to live side by side with equal respect and equal rights, then you move the debate to more favourable territory (so to speak).[42]

Newsweek reported that 'the 18 chapters offer a fascinating look at the way Israel and its supporters try to shape the public debate in their favour'.[43]

The dictionary was created by leading US pollster Frank Luntz, a key adviser to the Republican Party. It tells supporters: 'No matter what you are asked, bridge to a productive pro-Israel message.' It says that the left in the United States believes that

> Israel is so rich and so strong that they fail to see why it is necessary for armoured tanks to shoot at unarmed kids. The pictures of Israeli troops firing on Palestinian children and Israeli tanks bulldozing Palestinian villages have created a deep and unfortunately

lasting impression of Israel as the aggressor in the current conflict.[44]

A section headlined 'Words that work' gives a form of words which, it says, will win applause everywhere—particularly from the left: 'The conditions of the Palestinians living in the West Bank and Gaza are unbelievably difficult. It is a catastrophe. We want to change it. Israel wants to change it.' It coaches supporters of Israel on how to avoid using the word 'settlement'. If asked will Israel dismantle settlements, the way to answer is with 'Peace is about more than land or borders. It is about jobs, prosperity and opportunity for all,' and it refers to the idea of evacuating Jews (settlers) from the West Bank as racist.

The Luntz document says that justifying the demolition of Palestinian homes on the grounds that they infringe Jerusalem's municipal rules does not work with Americans, who don't like local councils: 'Worse yet, talking about "violations of building codes" when a TV station is showing the removal of a house that looks older than the modern state of Israel is simply catastrophic.'

Finally, to the most important matter of all when it comes to language: the accusation of anti-Semitism cannot be used to shut down debate. In recent years in Australia we've seen some tough and confronting reporting of the Australian military. Mark Willacy, Dan Oakes and Sam Clark from the ABC, and Nick McKenzie and

Chris Masters from Nine, have revealed some horrible things done in the Australian uniform in Afghanistan. No-one could reasonably suggest that by doing this reporting they were being 'un-Australian'. Indeed, the majority of decent and professional soldiers in the Special Air Service—and they are the vast majority— wanted the truth to be told to preserve the integrity of their unit.

Likewise, the notion that anyone who criticises Israel or its army (or even former prime minister Benjamin Netanyahu) is being anti-Israeli or anti-Semitic is nonsense. Worse than that, in my view it's used way too often to try to scare the media away from reporting without fear or favour. I spoke to scores of senior journalists and editors for this book, and over and over I was told words to the effect: 'No editor wants to be accused of being anti-Semitic.'

The Australian media needs to get to a point where the reality of Israel can be discussed. Israelis have the facts. For instance, Israelis are able to read the views of more than 300 retired senior members of Mossad, Shin Bet, the Israeli army and the Israel Police who are part of a growing group called Commanders for Israel's Security. They have added up the combined time they have served in Israel's security agencies—9000 years. Arguing in support of 'two states for two peoples', the group dismisses outright the claim by the far right that Israel cannot support a Palestinian state because it would endanger the country's security:

There is no basis to the intimidating claims that a political arrangement will undermine security. The opposite is true! A political arrangement will enhance security. The IDF can provide an effective response to any security challenge, and its strength provides the Government of Israel with the negotiating space required to achieve peace arrangements.[45]

In Israel, that sort of statement is part of the dialogue, but if reported in Australia, that sort of news would be branded as biased, anti-Israel or anti-Semitic. One of the most eloquent recent warnings of the misuse of anti-Semitism came from former Australian foreign minister Gareth Evans in a letter to *The Sydney Morning Herald*:

Calling out China for its persecution of Uighurs is not to be a Sinophobic racist. Calling out Myanmar for its crimes against Rohingya people is not to be anti-Buddhist. Calling out Saudi Arabia and Egypt for their murder and suppression of dissidents is not to be Islamophobic or anti-Arab. And calling out Israel for its sabotage of the two-state solution, and creation of a de facto apartheid state, is not to be anti-Semitic.[46]

This is a point supported by Rupert Murdoch's former senior editor Chris Mitchell. He says that while there are, indeed, anti-Semites, the accusation of anti-Semitism is too often used to block debate.

Peter Greste agrees: 'While there will always be some journalism that is biased, by and large, Australian reporters do a pretty good job of covering the crisis with fairness and balance. What concerns me is the way that any reporting critical of Israel is so often condemned as being "anti-Semitic". The allegation of racism'—and because of the Holocaust, anti-Semitism is understood to be a particularly toxic form of racism—'places journalists in an impossible position where anything they report from that point on is going to be seen as biased. Another report that places Israel in a bad light will confirm the allegation of anti-Semitism, while a report favourable to Israel will be seen as caving in to Israeli pressure.' Greste adds: 'But playing the racism card is a cynical way of misdirecting attention from uncomfortable journalism to the journalists themselves, and ultimately undermines the value of good reporting and public debate.'

Philippe Agret says he believes Israel's endgame is Eretz Israel. The global picture, he says, is 'Let's do it progressively, gradually, quietly, building, building, building. We cannot get Nablus, so let's leave Nablus a Bantustan. We cannot get parts of Hebron, so let's leave Hebron as a Bantustan.'

It is Agret's next answer that shocks me. I ask him who is self-censoring in their reporting of Israel. Without hesitation, he replies: 'Everybody.'

Australians deserve better.

ACKNOWLEDGEMENTS

Enormous thanks to Louise Adler, who had the idea for this book and the determination to tackle an issue which many others assiduously avoid. My deep gratitude to the team at Monash University—particularly Vice-Chancellor Professor Margaret Gardner AC for inviting Louise Adler to commission the In the National Interest series, and to Paul Smitz for his great care with the manuscript and the project. And to Tom Molomby and Janet Bell, for their steadfast friendship and the time and effort they put into reading the drafts of this book as well as my previous book, *Balcony over Jerusalem*.

And an acknowledgment of all the brilliant colleagues with whom I've worked in my forty years in journalism, from my time as an eighteen-year-old cadet journalist at *The Herald* in Melbourne to *The Australian*, *The Bulletin*, the Nine Network, *The Sydney Morning Herald* and the ABC.

A special dedication to my wife, Sylvie Le Clezio, and our son Jack, who shared our wonderful six-year adventure in the Middle East—we travelled from Israel and Iran to Lebanon, Syria, Turkey, Morocco, Tunisia, Egypt and Saudi Arabia. And to Sylvie for her extraordinary assistance with this book. Her research, her deep knowledge of the issues involved, her grasp of detail and her fact-checking have made this a wonderful team effort.

NOTES

1 John Lyons, 'Stone Cold Justice', *Four Corners*, ABC, 10 February 2014, https://www.abc.net.au/4corners/stone-cold-justice-promo/5245064 (viewed July 2021).

2 Oren Kessler, 'Jodi Rudoren: Not Counting "Todahs", "Shukrans"', *The Jerusalem Post*, 17 February 2012, https://www.jpost.com/national-news/jodi-rudoren-not-counting-todahs-shukrans (viewed July 2021).

3 Chemi Shalev, 'A *New York Times* Reporter Is Invariably Called an Anti-Semite or Self-Hating Jew', *Haaretz*, 16 January 2014, https://www.haaretz.com/.premium-covering-israel-no-piece-of-cake-1.5312192 (viewed July 2021).

4 John Lyons, 'Stone Cold Justice', *The Weekend Australian Magazine*, 25 November 2011, https://www.theaustralian.com.au/life/weekend-australian-magazine/stone-cold-justice/news-story/832380779022d889cdb491120895b45c (viewed July 2021).

5 John Lyons, *Balcony over Jerusalem: A Middle East Memoir*, HarperCollins, Sydney, 2017, p. 185.

6 Patrick Kingsley, 'Evictions in Jerusalem become Focus of Israeli–Palestinian Conflict', *The New York Times*, 7 May 2021, https://www.nytimes.com/2021/05/07/world/middleeast/evictions-jerusalem-israeli-palestinian-conflict-protest.html (viewed July 2021).

7   Patrick Kingsley, 'A House Divided: A Palestinian, a Settler and the Struggle for East Jerusalem', *The New York Times*, 7 June 2021, https://www.nytimes.com/2021/06/07/world/middleeast/east-jerusalem-house-divided.html (viewed July 2021).

8   Military Court Watch: Monitoring the Treatment of Children in Israeli Military Detention, 'Fact Sheet', November 2019, https://www.militarycourtwatch.org/page.php?id=a6r85VcpyUa4755A52Y2mp3 (viewed July 2021).

9   The Association for Civil Rights in Israel, 'One Rule, Two Legal Systems: Israel's Regime of Laws in the West Bank', 24 November 2014, https://law.acri.org.il/en/2014/11/24/twosysreport (viewed July 2021).

10 Emma Green, 'Israel's New Law Inflames the Core Tension in Its Identity', *The Atlantic*, 21 July 2018, https://www.theatlantic.com/international/archive/2018/07/israel-nation-state-law/565712 (viewed July 2021).

11 Policy and Survey Research, 'The Palestinian/Israel Pulse, a Joint Poll', media release, 26 October 2020, http://pcpsr.org/en/node/824 (viewed July 2021).

12 Yoram Dinstein, *The International Law of Belligerent Occupation*, Cambridge University Press, Cambridge, 2009, p. 277.

13 Human Rights Watch, 'Israel: "Disengagement" Will Not End Gaza Occupation', 28 October 2004, https://www.hrw.org/news/2004/10/28/israel-disengagement-will-not-end-gaza-occupation (viewed July 2021).

14 Chaim Levinson, 'Israel Has 101 Different Types of Permits Governing Palestinian Movement', *Haaretz*, 23 December 2011, https://www.haaretz.com/1.5222134?lts=1625383550626 (viewed July 2021).

15 *The Times of Israel*, 'Leading Critic of French Al-Dura Coverage Convicted', 26 June 2013, https://www.timesofisrael.com/leading-critic-of-french-al-dura-coverage-convicted (viewed July 2021).

16 Greg Sheridan, 'Evil and Deeply Untrue', *The Australian*, 1 March 2014, https://www.theaustralian.com.au/national-affairs/opinion/evil-and-deeply-untrue/news-story/80a40debe2610c84bc86ab8374c6edbf (viewed July 2021).

17 John Lyons, 'Distant "Experts" Chose to Ignore Israeli Realities', *The Australian*, 8 March 2014, https://www.theaustralian.com.au/news/world/distant-experts-choose-to-ignore-israeli-realities/news-story/cdcaf2a426bba32ca6745d918b60588d (viewed July 2021).

18 Greg Sheridan, 'Rise of Anti-Semitism Must Not Be Israeli Leader's Lasting Legacy', *The Australian*, 5 June 2021, https://www.theaustralian.com.au/inquirer/rise-of-antisemitism-must-not-be-israeli-leader-netanyahus-lasting-legacy/news-story/0044d67f52b859b61b93d0640a7ba51c (viewed July 2021).

19 Email from ABC Corporate Affairs to Samah Sabawi, 16 September 2020.

20 Do Better on Palestine, 'Open Letter from Journalists, Media Workers, Writers and Commentators', 14 May 2021, https://dobetteronpalestine.com (viewed July 2021).

21 Evan Zlatkis, 'Probe into SMH, Age, "Palestine" Crossword', *The Australian Jewish News*, 9 September 2019, https://ajn.timesofisrael.com/probe-into-palestine-crossword (viewed July 2021).

22 Medialetterpalestine.medium.com, 'An Open Letter on U.S. Media Coverage of Palestine', 9 June 2021, https://medialetterpalestine.medium.com/an-open-letter-on-u-s-media-coverage-of-palestine-d51cad42022d (viewed July 2021).

23 David M Halbfinger and Adam Rasgon, 'Life under Occupation: The Misery at the Heart of the Conflict', *The New York Times*, 22 May 2021, https://www.nytimes.com/2021/05/22/world/middleeast/israel-gaza-conflict.html (viewed July 2021).

24 Dahlia Scheindlin, 'Israel Is Falling Apart, because the Conflict Controls Us', *The New York Times*, 20 May 2021, https://www.nytimes.com/2021/05/20/opinion/Israel-palestine-netanyahu-gaza.html (viewed July 2021).

25 Isabel Kershner, 'Israel Says Actions in Gaza Not War Crimes', *The New York Times*, 22 April 2009, https://www.nytimes.com/2009/04/23/world/middleeast/23gaza.html (viewed July 2021).

26 John Lyons, *Balcony over Jerusalem: A Middle East Memoir*, HarperCollins, Sydney, 2017, p. 254.

27 Ibid., p. 252. 'The stories you did on Palestinian children' refers to: John Lyons, 'Stone Cold Justice', *The Weekend Australian Magazine*, 25 November 2011.

28 Chris Mitchell, *Making Headlines*, Melbourne University Press, Melbourne, 2016.

29 J-Wire, 'Rudd to Lead Largest Ever Delegation to Israel', 27 October 2010, https://www.jwire.com.au/rudd-to-lead-largest-ever-delegation-to-israel (viewed July 2021).

30 Kevin Toolis, 'Young, Bright and Ready to Blow Herself to Pieces', *The Advertiser*, 7 October 2006.

31 Maher Mughrabi, 'Prisoner Swap Unequal to Task', *The Sydney Morning Herald*, 25 October 2011, https://www.smh.com.au/politics/federal/prisoner-swap-unequal-to-task-20111024-1mg9g.html (viewed July 2021).

32 The Mayne Report, 'Transcript from Fairfax AGN, Debate on Middle East Coverage', 24 October 2010, https://web.archive.org/web/20110113150942/www.maynereport.com/articles/2010/11/24-1309-3462.html (viewed July 2021).

33 JTA, 'Anti-Israel Cartoon Breaches Australian Press Code', *The Times of Israel*, 21 January 2015, https://www.timesofisrael.com/anti-israel-cartoon-breaches-australian-press-code (viewed July 2021).

34 *The Sydney Morning Herald*, 'We Apologise: Publishing Cartoon in Original Form Was Wrong', 3 August 2014, https://www.smh.com.au/national/we-apologise-publishing-cartoon-in-original-form-was-wrong-20140803-zzxab.html (viewed July 2021).

35 Ed O'Loughlin, 'Wars between Worlds', *The Age*, 10 May 2008, https://www.theage.com.au/world/wars-between-worlds-20080510-ge7272.html (viewed July 2021).

36 Do Better on Palestine, 'Open Letter from Journalists, Media Workers, Writers and Commentators', 14 May 2021, https://dobetteronpalestine.com (viewed July 2021).

37 Steve Linde, 'Staying Jewish Down Under', *The Jerusalem Post*, 29 October 2016, https://www.jpost.com/magazine/staying-jewish-down-under-468989 (viewed July 2021).

38 Oliver Holmes, 'Israel Is Committing the Crime of Apartheid, Rights Group Says', *The Guardian* (Australian edn), 27 April 2021, https://www.theguardian.com/world/2021/apr/27/israel-committing-crime-apartheid-human-rights-watch (viewed July 2021).

39 Human Rights Watch, 'A Threshold Crossed: Israeli Authorities and the Crimes of Apartheid and Persecution', 27 April 2021, https://www.hrw.org/report/2021/04/27/threshold-crossed/israeli-authorities-and-crimes-apartheid-and-persecution (viewed July 2021).

40 Ibid.

41 *The Forward* and JJ Goldberg, '106 Retired Generals, Spy Chiefs Urge Netanyahu to Push for Peace', *Haaretz*, 3 November 2014, https://www.haaretz.com/ex-spies-urge-bibi-to-pursue-peace-1.5323633 (viewed July 2021).

42 The Israel Project, *The Israel Project's 2009 Global Language Dictionary*, 2009, https://www.transcend.org/tms/wp-content/uploads/2014/07/sf-israel-projects-2009-global-language-dictionary.pdf (viewed July 2021).

43 *Newsweek*, 'How to Sell Americans on Israeli Settlements', 9 July 2009, https://www.newsweek.com/how-sell-americans-israeli-settlements-81783 (viewed July 2021).

44 The Israel Project, *The Israel Project's 2009 Global Language Dictionary*, 2009, https://www.transcend.org/tms/wp-content/uploads/2014/07/sf-israel-projects-2009-global-language-dictionary.pdf (viewed July 2021).

45 Commanders for Israel's Security, 'Members', 2021, http://en.cis.org.il/members (viewed July 2021).

46 Gareth Evans, 'Not Anti-Semitic', *The Sydney Morning Herald* ('Letters' section), 14 June 2021, https://www.smh.com.au/national/nsw/reliance-on-migrant-labour-exposes-slothful-selfishness-20210613-p580ls.html (viewed July 2021).

IN THE NATIONAL INTEREST

Other books on the issues that matter:

Bill Bowtell *Unmasked: The Politics of Pandemics*

Michael Bradley *System Failure:*
The Silencing of Rape Survivors

Samantha Crompvoets *Blood Lust, Trust & Blame*

Rachel Doyle *Power & Consent*

Wayne Errington & Peter van Onselen
Who Dares Loses: Pariah Policies

Kate Fitz-Gibbon *Our National Shame:*
Violence against Women

Paul Fletcher *Governing in the Internet Age*

Jill Hennessy *Respect*

Richard Marles *Tides that Bind: Australia in the Pacific*

Fiona McLeod *Easy Lies & Influence*

Louise Newman *Rape Culture*

Martin Parkinson *A Decade of Drift*

Abul Rizvi *Population Shock*

Kevin Rudd *The Case for Courage*

Don Russell *Leadership*

Scott Ryan *Challenging Politics*

Kate Thwaites & Jenny Macklin *Enough Is Enough*

Simon Wilkie *The Digital Revolution: A Survival Guide*